PRACTICAL TRUTHS
FROM
FIRST
THESSALONIANS

by
F.E. Marsh
Foreword by
Howard F. Sugden

KREGEL PUBLICATIONS
Grand Rapids, Michigan 49501

Library of Congress Cataloging-in-Publication Data

Marsh, F.E. (Frederick Edward), 1858-1919.
  Practical Truths From First Thessalonians.

  Reprint. Originally published: Flashes From the
Lighthouse of Truth. Stirling [Scotland]: Drummond's
Tract Depot, [n.d.]
  1. Bible. N.T. Thessalonians, 1st—Sermons.
2. Sermons, English. I. Marsh F.E. (Frederick Edward),
1858-1919. Flashes From the Lighthouse of Truth.
II. Title.
BS2725.4.M37 1986   227'.8106   86-2742
ISBN 0-8254-3234-0

Printed in the United States of America

CONTENTS

FOREWORD

It was almost half a century ago that God, in His concern for my understanding of His word and the development of my Christian faith and life, dropped a priceless volume in my hands, by an author whose name was F. E. Marsh.

From that day to this it has been my pleasure and profit to have a growing acquaintance with this remarkable man of God. Frequently, I take from my shelves an autographed copy of one of the volumes that came from his pen eighty-five years ago. The wonder of that volume always stirs new desires and hopes, and kindles a flame of devotion upon the altar of my heart.

When "Practical Truths From First Thessalonians" (formerly "Flashes From the Lighthouse of Truth") was brought to my attention, I was excited, because here was a volume I had never had the privilege of seeing, let alone the opportunity of studying. Immediately, I began a walk through the first three chapters of the epistle of First Thessalonians. Marsh offers twenty-seven chapters of choice exposition. In this volume there is a wealth of enrichment for our spiritual lives. Herein a truly great teacher carries us to heights where flashes of truth illuminate our minds.

I am personally grateful that this volume has been made available for pastors, teachers, and the Christian community; and I pray for its wide acceptance.

DR. HOWARD F. SUGDEN

South Baptist Church
Lansing, Michigan

PREFACE

THE following Bible Readings are notes of addresses given to the church at Bethesda Free Chapel, Sunderland. These notes are not a verbatim reproduction of the addresses *as* they were delivered, as I neither commit to memory, nor read my addresses, but they form the *basis* of what was said. The reason for my publishing " Flashes from the Lighthouse of Truth " is three-fold. First, in answer to many requests to publish a book of my Bible Readings. Second, as an illustration of what I believe to be the need of the pulpit to-day (although it may seem egotistical for me to say it), namely, simple, illustrative, expository preaching. Third, that many of the Lord's people may be helped in the Divine life, through being led to a more thorough, patient, prayerful study of God's Word, for this is the secret of abiding com-munion with the Father and the Son, in the Holy Spirit.

F. E. MARSH

PRACTICAL TRUTHS
FROM
FIRST THESSALONIANS

" Paul, and Silvanus, and Timothy, unto the Church of the Thessalonians in God the Father and the Lord Jesus Christ" **(1 Thess. 1:1 R.V.)**

1

COMPANIONS IN LABOR
AND THE CHURCH

AMONG the many places that the Apostle Paul visited during his second missionary journey was Thessalonica, as we have recorded in Acts 17. Thessalonica lies at the northeastern corner of the Thermaic Gulf, on the line of the great Egnatian road, which formed the main connection by land between Italy and the East. From this it may be gathered that it was an important place. Its present name is Saloniki. Thessalonica is supposed to have been built on the site of the ancient Therma, or peopled from this city by Cassander, son of Antipater, and named after his wife Thessaloniki, sister of Alexander the Great. But we have to do with the Church at Thessalonica, and not the place. The First Epistle to the Church at Thessalonica written from Corinth about A.D. 52 or 54.

I. The companions in labour. — "Paul, and Silvanus, and Timothy." To mention the names of some men is at once to suggest a leading trait in

their character. It is so with the above devoted
servants of God. We characterize them as follows:
Paul the gracious, Silvanus the helpful, and Timothy
the faithful.

1. *Paul the gracious.* Paul was gracious because
he was *graced.* No one was more ready to acknowledge his indebtedness to the grace of God than Paul.
Whether in salvation, service, or suffering his
testimony is, "Yet not I, but the grace of God"
(1 Cor. xv. 10). The grace of God to Paul was as a
refreshing stream, which had cleansed away all the
filth of his past life, and slaked and satisfied the
burning thirst of his unsatisfied heart. The grace of
God to Paul was as a *beautiful dress,* which had
covered all his defects and deformities, and made him
graced and glorious in the Beloved (Eph. i. 6). As
the garments of glory and beauty made the high
priest glorious, so Paul was graced in the perfection
of Christ. The grace of God to Paul was as a *mighty
force,* which electrified his whole being, and made
him strong to suffer, serve, and sympathize.

Paul was gracious, because he was *godly.* The
man who knows the grace of God becomes like the
God of grace. When Paul was at Ephesus God did
special miracles through him, and among the rest
was to cast demons out of those who were possessed
by them. When some of the Jews saw this they
tried to do the same. They thought there was some
magic art in the mention of the name of Jesus; they
therefore used that name in commanding demons to
come out of those possessed. What was the result?
The evil spirit answered them, "Jesus I know, and Paul

I know; but who are ye? And the man in whom the evil spirit was, leaped on them, and overcame them, and prevailed against them, so that they fled out of that house naked and wounded" (Acts xix. 11-16). How did the evil spirit know Paul? Because God through Paul had already done damage to the realm of the evil one. Why was it God could use Paul? It was because he was in touch with God. A godly man is one who is walking in habitual communion with God. As the handles of an electric machine are unable of themselves to communicate the electricity that is in the battery, so neither has any man, naturally, power to communicate that which is Divine; but as the electric current, when it is applied, flows through the handles of the machine, and electrifies the one who touches them, so the believer who is in touch with God, being possessed by Him, has power with men and demons, because the power of God possesses him. We have power, as the power of God has us. We must *be*, to do.

2. *Silvanus the helpful.* The helpfulness of Silvanus—or, as he is more generally named, *Silas*—is seen in two ways. First, in that he stood with Paul in the time of persecution; and second, because he strengthened young believers. Silas did not desert his companion in the time of persecution, as we see when they were set upon at Philippi. A man, who had already hazarded his life for the sake of his Lord (Acts xv. 26), was not likely to leave one of His servants at such a time. We sometimes wonder whether the prison at Philippi would have heard that midnight song if Silas had not been with Paul.

Anyway we may judge that the one encouraged the other, till at last they break forth in glad song in praising God. We can almost imagine we hear them chanting the 103rd Psalm.

Again, Silas was specially helpful in that he strengthened the young converts who had been brought to Christ. Twice do we read the significant words, " It pleased Silas to abide there still" (Acts xv. 34; xvii. 14). Thus it is said of him, when he was at Antioch and Berea. Undoubtedly he tarried behind to confirm the young believers by ministering to them the Word of God, for we read, " Silas . . . exhorted the brethren with many words, and confirmed them . . . preaching the Word of the Lord" (Acts xv. 32-35). Silas was a true helper in the work of the Gospel, in that he watered what others had planted.

3. *Timothy the faithful.* The faithfulness of Timothy is manifest, in that he was faithful to the Word of God, and faithful in the work of God. He was *faithful to the Word of God.* Paul says of him, in speaking of himself and Silas as to the manner and matter of their preaching, " The Son of God, Jesus Christ, who was preached among you by us, even by me and Silvanus and Timotheus, was not yea and nay, but in Him was yea" (2 Cor. i. 19). There was no blowing hot and cold with the same breath. They did not preach one thing one time, and knock it down the next. And in thus declaring his own faithfulness and that of Silas, in keeping to the truth of God, he also commended Timothy for the same thing in coupling his name with theirs.

Again, Timothy was *faithful in the work of God.* There is no doubt in our minds as to the devotion of Paul in the service of God, and there can be none as to Timothy, for he speaks of him in such terms as the following: "Timotheus, my workfellow" (Rom. xvi. 21). "Timotheus . . worketh the work of the Lord, as I also do" (1 Cor. xvi. 10). "Timotheus . . I have no man like-minded, who will naturally care for your state" (Philip. ii. 19, 20). "Timotheus, our brother, and minister of God, and our fellow-labourer in the Gospel of Christ" (1 Thess. iii. 2). Timothy had plenty of ballast, because he was freighted with the truth of God; there was no insubordination in the vessel of his being, for he was under the control of the Spirit of God; and he was yoked with Christ in holy service, hence the reason of his faithfulness.

These three servants of God, who had been used by God in planting the Church at Thessalonica, remind us of the three graces—faith, hope, and love. Love is seen in Paul, hope in Silas, and faith in Timothy. The love of God seems to be shining upon Paul, like the sun at noonday, till it permeates the whole of his being, and makes him glow with the holy passion of love to Christ, with an ardent desire to please his Lord, a pressing forward to apprehend his glorified Saviour in His resurrection power, and a longing to be with the Divine Lover of his soul. Hope, like an anchor, keeps Silas steady in his testimony for Christ. He is not influenced by the storms of sin and error that beat around him, hence he is able to hold others, because he is held by Christ. Faith, like an armour, covers Timothy. Being thus in the panoply of God, and energized in the strength of God, he goes forth to fight the good fight of faith. These three brethren now send greeting to the Church at Thessalonica, and we can well conceive with what joy the Church would welcome this letter from their spiritual fathers.

II. THE CHURCH IN GOD, &c.—"The Church of the Thessalonians in God the Father and the Lord Jesus Christ." The following trio of points are suggested by the above words:—relationship, receptivity, and responsibility.

1. *Relationship.* All men are in God as His creatures, as dependent upon Him for natural life (Acts xvii. 28), but it is only those who are children of God through the begetting of the Holy Spirit (James i. 18; 1 Peter i. 23), and faith in Christ (Gal. iii. 26), of whom it can be said that they "are in God the *Father.*" As one has said, "Now, as in the Apostolic age, there are persons who are Christians, and persons who are not; and however alike their lives may be on the surface, they are radically apart. Their centre is different; the element in which they move is different; the nutriment of thought, the fountain of motives, the standard of purity, are different; they are related to each other as life in God, and life without God; life in Christ, and life apart from Christ; and in proportion to their sincerity is their antagonism."

Being "in God the Father" is consequent upon being "in the Lord Jesus Christ." And mark, it is not merely "in Christ," as in many places, but "in the Lord Jesus Christ." The full title of the Lord is given, and this full title connects His authority with His manhood and glory. Thus to be *in* the Lord Jesus Christ means to be in Him *as* Lord Jesus Christ. In Him as Lord *Jesus* Christ, that is, in Him as saved by Him, and identified with Him in His life, death, and resurrection, thus to experience His ability not only to save *from* the uttermost of what we deserve, but *to* the uttermost of His purpose. In Him as Lord Jesus *Christ*, as the anointed One at God's right hand, and as the anointing One who gives the Holy Spirit for life and labour. And in Him as *Lord* Jesus Christ, as slaves in the household, who love their Lord, and gladly do His bidding.

2. *Receptivity.* " Ye in Me, and I in you," said Christ. " Ye in Me," He seems to say—" that is your position; and I in you—that is your power." The one is the counterpart and consequence of the other, as the iron being in the fire, the fire is in the iron. A man cannot be as a house with doors and windows closed against the light, yet standing in the midst of light. A ship may take refuge in a harbour without receiving any one on board or sending any one ashore ; but a man cannot so deal with God : he cannot take refuge in God without letting God in. The diver goes down into the water to find treasure, but carefully excludes the water ; a man cannot so deal with God and the treasures hid in God. In the very act of finding safety and rest in God, he must open his soul to God. In God the Father as an *Habitation*, thus to receive of His provision and

protection. In God the Father as a *Home*, thus to participate in its rest and refreshment. In the *love* of God the Father, thus to love with His love. In the *life* of God the Father, thus to live as He commands. In the *Lord* Jesus Christ, thus to do all at His direction, under His supervision, and for His glory. In the Lord *Jesus* Christ, thus to know His power to save to the uttermost, whether as to time, trial, or temptation. And in the Lord Jesus *Christ*, thus to be in the atmosphere of His presence for communion, and for Him to be in us in His holiness and graciousness.

3. *Responsibility.* Our responsibility is suggested by several things. Being in God the Father, as His children, we are responsible to obey Him. Being in the Lord Jesus Christ, we are called upon to yield ourselves to Him. And being in the Church, we must be true to the position we occupy as members of it. We refer to the latter as indicating our responsibility. The meaning of the word " Church " is " assembly." We read of the "Church (assembly) in the wilderness" (Acts vii. 38); and of the assembly (Church) at Ephesus (Acts xix. 32); but here there is a special qualification, it is " the Church in God," &c. " It is not civic, but religious; though religious, it is neither pagan nor Jewish. It is an original creation, new in its bond of union, in the law by which it lives, in the objects at which it aims." The Church of God, by virtue of its relationship to the Father, and the Lord Jesus Christ, occupies a position which is distinct from all other. As the assembly in the wilderness was separate from the surrounding nations,

and had separate laws given to it, so the Church of God is set apart to God from the world, and is responsible to be true to Him who is her author and Head, by keeping the position in which He has placed her, and to obey His Word in all things.

" Grace to you, and peace " (1 Thess. 1:1 R.V.)

2

A COUPLET OF BLESSINGS

THE couplet of blessings which is contained in the above salutation of the servants of Christ, who had been the means, in God's hand, of founding the Church at Thessalonica, is like two noble and carved pillars in a building, which give strength and beauty to it. This greeting comprehended all that the Greek meant by his "grace," and all that the Hebrew conveyed by his "peace;" and much more, for the grace and peace come from God.

All the Epistles of Paul, excepting that to the Hebrews, have a like salutation; and the pastoral Epistles of Paul to Timothy and Titus have the addition of "mercy" to "grace" and "peace," which is placed between the two latter. We might say of this trio of blessings that they represent love in action; for grace is love bestowing its favours upon the undeserving, mercy is love receiving the penitent, and peace is love in communion with the believer.

We shall look at the two graces which make the couplet of blessings in our passage, separately and conjointly.

I. THE COUPLET OF BLESSINGS VIEWED SEPARATELY.

—First grace, and then peace.

1. *Grace.*   Grace is the *action of love*, as seen in the Person of Christ—He is called "the Arm of Jehovah" (Isaiah liii. 1)—at work for the salvation of men, procuring for them, in His death and resurrection, life and liberty, so that God's free favour might be proclaimed to all; hence we hear of "the Gospel of the grace of God" (Acts xx. 24).   Grace is the *legacy of love* that gives to the believer untold and lasting wealth; hence we are reminded that the manner and measure of God's dealings are "according to the riches of His grace" (Eph. i. 7).   Grace is the *outflow of love,* in saving the undeserving, which comes to them as the water out of the rock to the murmuring Israelites in the wilderness; hence we read of the "God of grace" and the "grace of God" (Eph. ii. 5; 1 Peter v. 10).   Grace is the *strength of love,* which comes and removes the barriers which the sinner's sin had raised, and which kept God from the sinner, and the sinner from God; hence we are directed to the "throne of grace," where we can find mercy and grace to help in time of need (Heb. iv. 16).   Grace is the *service of love,* which is like a mighty flowing river, bearing on its bosom the heavily laden barges of God's goodness and truth to meet our every need; hence we are pointed to the "abundance of His grace" (Rom. v. 17).   Grace is the *passport of love,* which gives us the right to enter the King's treasury of "His exceeding great and precious promises," and to find whatever we want in Christian life and service; hence we find the "manifold grace of God" (1 Peter iv. 10).   Grace is the *might of love,* which causes the believer to be moved, as the water moves the mill-

wheel to grind the corn for the use of man, in graciousness of action towards others, and to be of use in serving others at all times; hence we know " the exceeding grace of God" (2 Cor. ix. 14).

"Grace to you." *The grace of the Father;* that we may learn the lessons He teaches. They are—*godliness* towards Himself, that we may prove we are His children; for as the child speaks of his parent by his likeness to him, so we evidence our relationship to God by the similarity of action; *sobriety* with reference to ourselves, that is, self-restraint, under the government of Christ, as faithful stewards who keep things in order, although others tempt us to do otherwise; *righteousness* in connection with our dealings with others; no unjust weight, no crooked action, no taking advantage of another's weakness or ignorance. These are the three lessons that grace teaches according to Titus ii. 11, 12.

The grace of the Son; that we may imitate Him in His actions. Think of the grace that was poured into His lips (Psalm xlv. 2), and evidenced by the gracious words that fell from them (Luke iv. 22). See the grace He manifested in His life in all His dealings with others—amidst trial, when persecuted, in His death, and in what He gave up. Well might the Apostle say, in exhorting the Church at Corinth to abound in the grace of giving, "For ye know the grace of our Lord Jesus Christ, that, though He was rich, yet for your sakes He became poor, that ye through His poverty might be rich" (2 Cor. viii. 9).

The grace of the Holy Spirit; that His power may rest upon us for walk and witnessing. "Great grace was upon them all " (Acts iv. 33), it is said of the early Christians after they were empowered by the Holy Spirit. The grace of the Spirit is as fire, to burn up all that is unholy, selfish, worldly, and mean; and is as the sap in the vine, to cause us to be fruitful branches, yielding the ninefold cluster of the " fruit of the Spirit."

2. *Peace.* The peace of the Gospel is not, as the Eastern salutation too often is, a mere empty form, as our " Good morning," but an abiding reality, which comes to us from the throne of God, by way of the cross of Christ, and is brought to us by the Holy Spirit. This peace is, as one has said, " The peace which Christ is; the peace with God which we have when we are reconciled to Him by the death of His Son; the soul-health which comes when grace makes our hearts, to their very depths, right with God, and frightens away care and fear. This spiritual soundness is all summed up in the Word." We note three characteristics of this blessing:—

(1) It is a *purchased* peace (Col. i. 20). The meaning of the word "peace" is suggestive, it signifies *that which binds together.* Sin severed man from God. God in justice must punish sin. Man must be for ever separated from God if His claims are not met. Christ steps in as the Mediator. He is One with God, therefore has the power to meet our liabilities and bear our penalties; and He is One with man, therefore has the right to take up our cause, and His actions are our actions, for with Him we are identified. This He does by making peace by the blood of His cross; thus peace being made by the

death of Christ, we have " peace with God" through
Him (Rom. v. 1).

(2) It is a *personified* peace. " He is our Peace "
(Eph. ii. 14). It is not merely *what* we receive, but
whom. It is not only peace from Christ, but Christ
as our Peace, that we possess. " In Pitti Palace, at
Florence, there are two pictures which hang side by
side, one representing a stormy sea with its wild
waves, and black clouds, and fierce lightnings flashing
across the sky. In the waters a human face is seen,
wearing an expression of the utmost agony and
despair. The other picture also represents the sea,
tossed by as fierce a storm, with as dark clouds ; but
out on the midst of the waves a rock rises, against
which the waters dash in vain. In a cleft of a rock
are some tufts of grass and green herbage, with sweet
flowers, and amid these a dove is seen sitting on her
nest, quiet and undisturbed by the wild fury of the
storm." Christ is the Rock of Ages. On Him we
rest, in Him we hide, and with Him we are safe.
Having Christ as our Peace, we have calm in the
midst of storm ; rest, while all around is raging ; and
joy in sorrow.

(3) It is a *protecting* peace. " The peace of God,
which passeth all understanding, shall keep your
hearts and minds through Christ Jesus" (Philip. iv. 7).
This promise is given to those who are not anxious
about anything, prayerful in everything, and thankful
for anything. These shall be kept by the peace of God
as with a garrison. The peace of God shall keep the
heart from fear, the mind from doubt, the thoughts
from wandering, the imagination from impurity, the

soul from strife, the spirit from carking care, and oneself from straying. As Matthew Henry says, " The peace of God will keep us from sinning under our troubles, and from sinking under them." The peace of God elevates to the God of peace, who shall keep from the dust of worldliness, from the mud spots of the flesh, and from the snares of the enemy, and cause us to know that He can sanctify us wholly, so that no part of our being shall be untouched by Him, but all shall be like a well-tuned instrument, upon which He can play to His praise.

II. THE COUPLET OF BLESSINGS VIEWED CON-JOINTLY.—" Grace and peace." Some seventeen times we find these coupled together in the Epistles; so their connection cannot be accidental, neither is the order in which they are mentioned. It is not peace and then grace, but grace and then peace. Grace is the cause of peace, and peace is the result of grace. Grace is the root of peace, and peace is the flower of grace. There is no true peace before we know grace, but there may be grace and yet not peace, just as there may be a flowerless plant.

Peace and sin will not live together. As Watson says, " If you would have peace, make war with sin. Sin is the Achan that troubles us, the Trojan horse. When Joram saw Jehu, he said, ' Is it peace, Jehu ?' and he answered, 'What peace, so long as the whore-doms of thy mother Jezebel and her witchcrafts are so many?' (2 Kings ix. 22). What peace, so long as sin remains unmortified ? If you would have peace with God, break the league with sin ; give battle to sin, for it is a most just war. When Samson had slain the lion, there came honey out of the lion; so, by slaying sin, we get the honey of peace." It was after king Asa had cut down the groves of Baal, broken down the images, and sought the Lord, to keep His commandments, that we read, "The kingdom was quiet, . . . because the Lord had given him rest," yea, "rest on every side" (2 Chron. xiv. 5, 6, 7).

The peace of God is known, as grace reigns in the heart. As when the disciples were gathered in the upper room, with shut doors, Jesus appeared in their midst and said, "Peace be unto you;" so when the world with its pleasures, and self with its ambitions, are shut out of our hearts, Christ enters and takes full possession of our being; then He says in the restfulness of His word, in the stillness of His Spirit, and in the calmness of His presence, "Peace be unto you," "My peace I give unto you" (John xiv. 27). And as long as our Lord has possession of us, by our continued trust in Him, we shall enjoy the secret and sanctifying blessing of "perfect peace" (Is. xxvi. 3).

Peace is the result of communion with grace. As David Brainerd said, "Filling up our time with, and for God, is the way to rise up and lie down in peace. . . . I longed that my life might be filled with fervency and activity in the things of God. Oh the peace, the composure, and God-like serenity of such a frame! Heaven must differ from this only in degree, not in kind." Mark those words, "*Filling up our time with God is the way to . . . peace.*" Surely this is possible? It is. We may have fellowship with God in all our life, whether it be our business life, home life, church life, social life, or private life, for it is as we have communion with God in all things, by doing all according to His Word, and for His glory, that the calm of God fills our spirit, like the storm-tossed lake that heard the stilling voice of Christ as He said, " Peace, be still," and at once was at rest.

THANKFULNESS AND
PRAYERFULNESS

"We give thanks to God always for you all, making mention of you in our prayers" (1 Thess. 1:2 R.V.)

3
THANKFULNESS AND PRAYERFULNESS

AMONG the many things that gave strength and beauty to the Temple built by Solomon were the two magnificent pillars called "Jachin" and "Boaz." These names are suggestive; the former means, "He will establish," and the latter, "In Him is strength." As these two pillars were for strength and beauty, so there are two things that give power and ornament to the temple of our being, and these are thankfulness and prayerfulness. And as the two leading thoughts in the meaning of the names are strength and stability, so, confiding in God by prayer, we shall be strong in Him; and consecrated to God we shall truly express our thanks to Him, for thanksgiving cannot be severed from thanksliving, and these characterizing us denote stability. Praise and prayer are like two buttresses to the Christian life. In fact, there is no spiritual life where these are lacking, for prayer is the voice of the quickened one that makes known its petition to God in the name of Jesus; and praise is the sacrifice which the believer offers up to God for blessings received and good bestowed. Thus it is not without significance and suggestion that the word " grace " mentioned in verse 1 is the same that is rendered in 1 Cor. xv. 57 " thanks." The first is grace toward us, blessing us with peace, and the second is grace within us, blessing God in praise.

I. THANKFULNESS. —" We give thanks to God always for you all." Praise should always have the precedence and predominance in our approach to God. Daniel prayed to the Lord *three* times a day, but the Psalmist said that he would praise God *seven* times in the day (Dan. vi. 10; Psalm cxix. 164). There are many things for which we find the Apostle Paul thanking God. Two characteristic expressions are, " Thanks be to God," and " I thank God." Four times does he use the words, " Thanks be to God :"— for the gift of Christ (2 Cor. ix. 15); for victory through Christ (1 Cor. xv. 57); for triumph in Christ (2 Cor. ii. 14); and for service to Christ, as illustrated in the care and interest that Titus manifested toward the Church at Corinth (2 Cor. viii. 16). But the causes of the thanksgiving of Paul and his fellow-labourers in writing to the Church at Thessalonica were special,—namely, the reality of their faith in Christ as seen in their work ; their love to Christ as manifest in their labour; and their hope in Christ as evidenced in their patience.

To thank God for what He does for, in, and through others is *healthful*. It indicates a good state of soul. We bring the thermometer of God's truth into the atmosphere of some Christian's lives, and immediately the mercury falls to the freezing point of jealousy, for they cannot delight in the success of others. At once we know that they are not in touch with the Lord, for, if they were, the green monster of jealousy would not be tolerated. Others are at the blood-heat of indifference. They are neither interested nor envious.

But those who are living in the atmosphere of God's presence delight in the advances and successes of others. As the father delights in his boy while he watches the progress he makes in the trade or profession to which he has placed him, so those honoured servants of Christ rejoiced in the Christian life and labour of the saints. In like manner we should be thankful when we behold believers making progress in the Divine life, when they are zealous in the Lord's service, and when they are successful in bringing others to Christ. For, if we do not, it is a sure sign that the clear shining of their lives reveals the dark spots in ours, and hence the reason of our not praising God for them.

Again, to thank God for others is *helpful.* Paul invariably began his Epistles by thanking God for the good and the grace that he saw in others (Rom. i. 8; 1 Cor. i. 4; Philip. i. 3; Col. i. 3; 2 Tim. i. 3-5; Philemon 4). There were things for which he had to chide some of the Churches, but he always thanked God for anything that was like Christ in them. Even when he had occasion to find fault, he generally prefaced his reproof by noting what called for commendation. Dr. Maclaren well says, " Gentle rain softens the ground and prepares it to receive the heavier downfall which would else mostly run off the hard surface. . . . These expressions . . . are the uncalculated and uncalculating expression of affection which delights to see white patches in the blackest character, and of wisdom which knows that the nauseous medicine of blame is most easily taken if administered wrapped in a capsule of honest praise." He futher remarks:—" It is nourishing food for many virtues, and a powerful antidote to many vices."

The Object of the thanksgiving. " Thanks be to *God.*" The Apostle is careful to thank *God* for the grace that he sees in and hears of others. As one has said, " This praise is cast in the form of thanksgiving to God as the true fountain of all that is good in man. How all that might be harmful in direct praise is strained out of it when it becomes gratitude to God ! . . . The fountain, not the pitcher filled from it, should have the credit of the crystal purity and sparkling coolness of the water." Every true child of God gratefully acknowledges that all good is from Him who alone can be called " Good ;" as the servant in the parable of the pounds confessed that it was the Lord's pound, with which he had been trading, that had gained the ten pounds.

The universality of the thanksgiving. " We give thanks for you *all.*" *All* were the cause for thanksgiving. There was no drawback. There was not one with whom fault was found. It was not so at Corinth, for there was a profane person (1 Cor. v. 13) who was a clog to the prosperity of the Church ; nor at Galatia, for Judaism, like a blight, had been introduced among them by troublers (Gal. v. 12) ; nor at Colosse, where there was a danger of dividing the glory that was due to Christ alone, by looking to angels and others (Col. ii. 18, 19). But at Thessalonica it was otherwise. There was no spot in their feast, no alloy in their gold. As the moon when full reflects the sun as it falls upon its surface, so these saints were walking in the full light of God's presence ; here was the reason of their thoroughness.

The continuance of the thanksgiving. "We give thanks to God *always* for you all." It was not sometimes that thanks had to be given for them, but always. Their life as believers, with its testimony, was not one in which a spasmodic effort was made at intervals, like the history of Israel as recorded in the book of Judges, which is a series of defeats and restorations ; but was as straight as a line and as steadfast as a rock. If we are always led in triumph by Christ through owning His rightful sway over us (2 Cor. ii. 14, R.V.), always abounding in the work of the Lord (1 Cor. xv. 58), always setting the Lord before us for our imitation (Psalm xvi. 8), praying always as dependent children (Eph. vi. 18), always ministering to our faith what the Lord enjoins (2 Peter i. 15), always obeying the truth (Philip. ii. 12), always rejoicing in the Lord (Philip. iv. 4), and always seeking to magnify Christ (Philip. i. 20), then there will be cause for thanks to God on our behalf always.

II. PRAYERFULNESS. "Making mention of you in our prayers." In praying for blessing upon others we bring blessing upon ourselves, just as the light in the lampstand in the tabernacle not only illuminated all in the holy place, but also gave light upon the lampstand itself, revealing its own beauty, as we read, " The seven lamps shall give light over against the candlestick " (Num. viii. 2).

Prayer for others extinguishes doubt and fear in ourselves. It may be said to be an axiom in the Christian life that those who are occupied with their own interests alone are very much like Mr. Fearing mentioned in *The Pilgrim's Progress.* " He was dejected at every difficulty, and stumbled at every straw that anybody cast in his way." Whereas, if he had sought to help others over their difficulties, he would have had no time for doubt and fear. We should be Greathearts, who are ever ready to lend a helping hand to others ; and one way we can do this is to do as Epaphras did for the saints at Colosse, who was " always striving for them in his prayers, that they might stand perfect· and fully assured in all the will of God " (Col. iv. 12, R.V.).

Prayer for others expresses a right state of soul in the pleader. It was Abraham, who was outside of Sodom, that pleaded with God on behalf of the wicked cities of the plain, and not Lot, who was inside Sodom. It was Moses who supplicated God for the murmuring Israelites, and stayed His hand in judgment thereby, and not Aaron, who, in an unguarded moment, granted the desire of the people in making the golden calf. As the indicator on the engine registers the amount of pressure within, so the interest we take in the welfare of others by praying for them is indicative of the state of our own spiritual life, for it is only the one who is walking with God that will be at leisure to turn to Him on the behalf of others.

Prayer for others empowers and increases our spiritual influence. That honoured servant of Christ, George Müller, has said, in bearing his testimony upon the power and influence of prayer to God on behalf of others, "There are ten persons for whom I have prayed daily for thirty years, and eight of them are converted; eighteen for whom I have prayed daily for twenty years, and fourteen of them are converted; and so on, with an increase in the number of persons and a decrease of results corresponding with the shortening of the time of intercession."

Prayer for others expands our sympathy. There are some who are so occupied with the little garden that is surrounded by the four walls of their sect or cause that they have no desire to see how their friends are doing next door, in order to do them a kindness by helping to pull up the weeds or to cultivate some plant of grace. If we seek by earnest prayer " to comprehend with *all saints,* what is the breadth, and length, and depth, and height " of Christ Himself, we shall find that that is one of the steps that will lead us into " the fulness of God " (Eph. iii. 18, 19).

Let us blend thankfulness with prayerfulness, for they are twins. The Holy Spirit exhorts us, " In everything by prayer and supplication, with thanksgiving, let your requests be made known unto God " (Philip. iv. 6). The following incident, which appeared in *The Christian* some time since, is full of touching interest :—

" A child knelt at the accustomed time to thank God for the mercies of the day, and pray for His care through the coming night.   Then, as usual, came the 'God bless mother and——.'   But the prayer was stifled, the little hands unclasped, and a look of sadness and wonder met the mother's eye, as the words of helpless sorrow came from the lips of the kneeling child, 'I cannot pray for father any more.'   Since her lips had been able to form that dear name she had prayed for a blessing upon it.   It had followed close after her mother's name.   But now he was dead.   I waited some moments and then urged her to go on.   Her pleading eyes met mine, and with a voice that faltered she said, 'O mother, I cannot leave him all out; let me say, "Thank God that I had a dear father once," so I can still go on and keep him in my prayers.'   And so she still continues to do, and my heart learned a lesson from the loving ingenuity of my child.   Remember to thank God for the mercies past as well as to ask blessings for the future."

THREE GRACES MAKING
THEMSELVES KNOWN

" Remembering without ceasing your work of faith and labour of love and patience of hope in our Lord Jesus Christ, before our God and Father " (1 Thess. 1:3 R.V.)

4
THREE GRACES
MAKING THEMSELVES KNOWN

THOMAS Adams, in speaking of the three graces, faith, hope, and love, says, "As the three principal colours of the rainbow — red, yellow, and blue, representing heat, light, and purifying power—supply in their combination all the other colours; so, by a sort of moral analysis, faith, hope, and love lie at the foundation, or enter into the composition of all other Christian excellencies. They are, in a word, inseparable graces. Faith always works by love, and these two virtues can wait patiently and hopefully for ultimate results. They are the crown of Christian believers, and the forces of the whole Church, and they must succeed. Faith says, 'I labour in the full confidence that I shall finally accomplish all I would;' love says, 'I delight in my work, and therefore will not slacken in my efforts until I have secured all I desire;' and hope says, 'I can wait patiently for all I joyfully anticipate.' These three graces are a created trinity, and have

some glimmering resemblance of the Trinity un-
create : for as the Son is begotten of the Father, and
the Holy Spirit proceeds from them both ; so here a
true faith begets a constant hope, and from them
proceeds love."

What are the graces, but the activity of grace
within us ?   Hence the grace of faith is from Him
who is the Object of faith, as the light of the moon
is the reflection of the light of the sun ; the grace of
love is from Him who is the Source of love, namely,
the One who is Love, as the water that is gathered
by the clouds from the sea, and cast into the rivulet
in the form of rain, flows back to that sea from whence
it came ; and the grace of hope is from Him who is
the God of hope, as the child owes its being to its
parents.

Faith looks back to the death of Christ, and rests
in His atonement for salvation, as the boards of the
tabernacle rested in and on the sockets of silver ;
love looks up to the person of Christ, and with gladness of heart exclaims, " I love Christ, because He
first loved me, and I will gladly do anything or
go anywhere for Him," as the maiden will leave home
and friends for him upon whom her affection is set ;
and *hope looks out* for the coming of Christ, as the
fisherman's wife waits in expectancy in the early
morning to hear the footfall of her beloved, who has
been toiling on the deep all night.

Faith is the hand that accepts the gift of God,
when Christ is offered in the preaching of the Gospel,
as the children of Israel in the wilderness took up
the water with their vessels, which was God's gift to

them in their need; *love is the heart* that beats with holy devotion to Christ in heroic actions, as illustrated in David's three mighty men, who, out of love to their king, broke through the host of the Philistines to obtain a drink of water from the well at Beth-lehem (1 Chron. xi. 18, 19); and *hope is the eye* that is looking forth into the darkness for the breaking of the dawn of day of Christ's approach, for the light of His coming shall change us into His image.

Faith is the grasp that lays hold of the shield of God's providing, and goes forth as a valiant soldier to do battle with sin and error; *love is the grace that lays up* treasure in heaven by unknown almsgiving, by ministering to the needs of others, by visiting the sick, by denying self in giving that which it had to others; and *hope is the girdle* that binds together the loins of the mind.   Thus we are strengthened to run the race, and to reach the goal.

Faith is the *telescope* that enables us to see the unseen realities of the kingdom, as the glass shows us numberless worlds in the heavens unseen by the naked eye; love is the *tie* that binds us to our Lord with cords that are stronger than death, mightier than the world, and more binding than any earthly relationship; and hope is the *traction* that causes us to live as strangers and pilgrims on the earth, and to be longing for the city whose Builder and Maker is God.

I. FAITH EVIDENCES ITSELF IN WORK.—" Work of faith."   Work is not the cause of faith, but faith is the cause of work.   There are many things that are said to be " of faith."   There is the " righteousness

of faith" (Rom. iv. 13), for it rests in the righteousness of God; there is the "word of faith" (Rom. x.
8), for that is the ground of its action; there is the
"spirit of faith" (2 Cor. iv. 13), for its disposition is
to believe; there is the "hearing of faith" (Gal. iii.
2, 5), for that is its attitude; there is the "shield of
faith" (Eph. vi. 16), for that is its protection; there
is the "joy of faith" (Philip. i. 25), for that is its gladness; there is the "steadfastness of faith" (Col. ii. 5),
for that is its stability; there is the "breastplate of
faith" (1 Thess. v. 8), for that is its shelter; there is
the "fight of faith" (1 Tim. vi. 12), for that is its
warfare; there is the "assurance of faith" (Heb. x.
22), for that is its confidence; there is the "prayer
of faith" (James v. 15), for that is its delight; there
is the "trial of faith" (1 Peter i. 7), for that is its
purifying; and there is the "work of faith" for that
is its occupation. Now the "work of faith"—or the
deed or the *business* of faith, as the word may be
rendered—manifests itself in the above ways, in the
different aspects of faith mentioned, for faith is the
mainspring of all. "In prayer, it is faith that makes
us successful; in obedience, it is faith that makes us
cheerful; in afflictions, it is faith that makes us
patient; in trials, it is faith that makes us resolute;
in desertions, it is faith that makes us comfortable;
in life, it is faith that makes us fruitful; and in
death, it is faith that makes us victorious." Every
one who reads that list of epitaphs in the West-
minster Abbey of the New Testament—the eleventh
chapter of the Epistle to the Hebrews, which tells
out the doings of faith in simple and striking words,

must be impressed with the influence that faith in God exerts. A friend said to Archbishop Whately on his death-bed, " The Lord has heard your prayers, and preserved your intellect unimpaired." He replied, " It is not intellect which can avail me now, but faith in Christ Jesus." We might add, it is not intellect that can avail anywhere, but faith in God will avail us always.

Faith in God is as a life-buoy that holds us up amid the raging waves of sin and the world, and enables us to lend a helping hand to others. It was faith that inspired the woman to anoint Christ with the costly ointment, and brought from Him the commendation, " She hath wrought a good *work* upon me " (Matt. xxvi. 10). So shall it be with us as we give Christ our best, our all, out of love to Himself; thus shall we prove our faith in Him.

II. LOVE MANIFESTS ITSELF IN LABOUR.—" Labour of love." The work of faith is positive, for it declares the reality and activity of faith; the labour of love is comparative, for it puts itself to trouble to accomplish its purpose. The former is the *effect* of faith in Christ, in that it demonstrates its presence by its action, as the sun is the cause of the rays of sunlight that fall upon us in their soothing warmth. The latter is the *effort* of love, which puts itself to inconvenience for the sake of others, as the good Samaritan did, when he went out of his way in caring for the man who fell among thieves. This will be seen at once if the words " work " and " labour " are noted. The first means " occupation, business;" and the second, " toil, hard work." There is all the difference between these words that is implied in the distinction between work and hard work. The word "labour" is used by Paul in declaring that he was often "in *weariness*" in his labours (2 Cor. xi. 27), and illustrations of it may be found in what Peter said when he told the Lord that he and his companions had "*toiled* all night and taken nothing*" (Luke v. 5); and also in the words used of Christ, when it said that He was "*wearied* with His journey" (John iv. 6). The word signifies "to be wearied by work," hence the "labour of love" denotes love tired out in its toil for others.

"A century ago, in the north of Europe, stood an old cathedral, upon one of the arches of which was a sculptured face of wondrous beauty. It was long hidden, until one day the sun's light striking through a slanted window revealed its matchless features. And ever after, year by year, upon the days when for a brief hour it was thus illuminated, crowds came and waited, eager to catch a glimpse of that face. It had a strange history. When the cathedral was being built, an old man, broken with the weight of years and care, came and besought the architect to let him work upon it. Out of pity for his age, but fearful lest his failing sight and trembling touch might mar some fair design, the master set him to work in the shadows of the vaulted roof. One day they found the old man asleep in death, the tools of his craft laid in order beside him, the cunning of his right hand gone, the face upturned to this marvellous face which he had wrought—the face of one whom he had loved and lost in early manhood. And when the artists and sculptors and workmen from all parts of the cathedral came and looked upon that face, they said, 'This is the grandest work of all; love wrought this.'"

What is there in our lives that shows the laboriousness of our love to Christ? How many aching heads, weary feet, tired bodies have we had for the sake of Christ in labouring for others? The labour of love is seen in ministering to those who are in need (Acts xx. 35; Heb. vi. 10); and in helping in the work of the Gospel (Rom. xvi. 6, 12; 1 Cor. xvi. 16; 1 Thess. v. 12; 1 Tim. iv. 10, v. 17; Rev. ii. 2, 3).

III. HOPE REVEALS ITSELF IN PATIENCE.— "Patience of hope in our Lord Jesus Christ." The usage of the word "hope" to-day is not the same as that in Scripture. The term in the Word of God is used to express something real and abiding, as an anchor in sure anchorage, which will not drag; but the word as commonly used now denotes something vague, and sometimes as visionary as the mirage in the desert. One is questioned as to his financial position, and he hopes he is all right, when he should be certain. Another is asked if he has peace with God, and he replies, "I hope so," when he should be sure. The hope of the Christian is founded upon the unalterable word of God, as in the case of Christ's promise when He pledged His word that He would come and receive His people to Himself; and the "*patience* of hope" signifies that we tenaciously cling to His word, as the ivy to the oak. For the "patience" of the New Testament is more than mere resignation: it denotes endurance, as illustrated in the tree which steadily grows and brings forth fruit (Luke viii. 15), and in the runner in the race, who perseveringly keeps on to the end (Heb. xii. 1). This is the attitude that believers in Christ should maintain—patiently waiting for the coming of the Lord.

"In the year 1683, Vienna, the capital of Austria, was besieged; a great army of Turks, who were then making war with the nations of Europe, lay before it. When it was known that they were near Vienna, the emperor of Austria fled from the city, and the poor people in it were left in sad fear and distress. The only person they thought likely to save them was the king of Poland, and they sent entreating him to come to their help. They knew that he could only come to them over the northern mountains, and day after day they rose early and watched for the first morning light, in the hope of seeing the Polish army on the mountains. It was anxious waiting, but hope sustained them. The siege began in July; on the 11th of September some weary watchers were looking out from the ramparts to the mountain of the Kalimburg, when—oh, delightful sight!—they saw something bright on the mountain-side, and discerned the lances and armour of the brave Poles marching to their rescue. That very day the battle was fought, the Turks defeated, and Vienna free." The Christian is surrounded by a worse enemy than ever the Austrians had, but there is no uncertainty with us as to the issue of the battle, as long as we abide in Christ. The warfare will soon be over, for our Lord is coming. Of this we are confident, for He has promised ; hence the " patience of hope " is " in " or " of our Lord Jesus Christ."

As the Apostle Paul and his companions tell the Church of the subject of their thanksgiving and prayers, caused by remembering their " work of faith," &c., they assure them it is not a mere formal matter with them, a passing commendation, nor is it an empty compliment which they send in their greeting : but the remembrance of them is made " before our God and Father," that is, in His presence. They seem to say, " Whenever we pray, we remember before God your faith, hope, and love. Our remembrance is one entertained in His presence, and in which His eye sees no insincerity." May we ever act *before God*, that is, in the consciousness of His presence ; not seeking to please men, but to please Him. Then when we thank God for our own blessings, and for His grace as manifest in others, it shall be done with gladness of heart, uprightness of spirit, purity of motive, and to the glory of God.

" Knowing, brethren beloved of God, your election "
(1 Thess. 1:4 R.V.)

5

ELECTION:
ITS CAUSE AND CONSEQUENCE

IN the course of conversation with a sister in Christ, as she was lying upon her bed, weak and suffering, she quoted the lines of a hymn that spoke of Christ's tender regard and sympathy as her Shepherd, and when she had finished she said, "Every word is full of meaning." We say the same as we ponder the verse that is the subject of our meditation. The words that make up this passage are like a string of pearls—each perfect in itself, and the whole making a beautiful necklace of truth. Mark the words:—

"Knowing." The knowledge of which mention is made is what the servants of God knew, and not what the Christians at Thessalonica apprehended. The knowledge here is the spiritual perception that gave them to see that God was carrying out His purpose through them, by the way the Gospel was accepted.

"Brethren." Union is indicated. The title "brethren" is more frequently used than any other name in denoting the oneness of believers in Christ with each other. It is a designation of endearment, which expresses the love that they have for each other.   Thus union and unity are implied in this appellation.

"*Beloved.*"   They were the objects of a peculiar affection, recipients of special grace.   Certainly they were not beloved for their own sake, their goodness' sake, or their works' sake.   It was for the sake of Him who is "the Beloved."   We are accepted and loved in the Beloved, because of the acceptableness of the Beloved; thus we become beloved as the Beloved —His name is ours.

"*Of God.*"   Here is the source of all blessing, the cause of our being loved, the reason of all—that believers are in Christ.   The Father is the *Embodiment* of love, for "God is Love."   Christ in His life, death, and person is the *Expression* of love, for He is God manifest in the flesh; and the Holy Spirit is the *Exhibitor* of love, for He it is who unfolds to us the love of God, and causes us to love.

"*Your election.*"   The Apostles knew that the believers at Thessalonica were beloved and elected of God for two reasons.   First, by the way in which the Gospel came and was received by them; and second, by the results that followed, as shown in their devotion to Christ, and their diligence in carrying out the Divine precepts.

The truth of election is one about which there are many misconceptions.   It may be well to give in a concise and clear form what the New Testament says about it; and then to show how it is illustrated in the Church before us.

There has been a great deal of unnecessary and unprofitable controversy regarding what are known as Calvinism and Arminianism.   But what saith the Scripture ?

I. THE CAUSE OF GOD'S CHOICE OF HIS PEOPLE IS IN HIMSELF, AND NOT IN THEM.—There are many things in the natural world in which analogy may be found of the spiritual; but it is not safe nor sound to say that in every case there is an identity of law in the natural and spiritual kingdoms; yet, in some instances it would be perfectly legitimate to say that there is an identity in both realms.   As a case in point, the child owes its being to its parents, independently of its own will and action; in like manner the child of God is begotten of God, apart from his works or will, for the very desire to become a believer in Christ, and a willingness to do anything for salvation, give evidence of the quickening of the Holy Spirit, as we have it illustrated on the day of Pentecost in the cry of those upon whom the Spirit had been working, " What shall we do ?"

We are able to arrive at a conclusion by reviewing the opposite at times; for instance, in noting what a man is not as a tradesman we narrow the circle as to what he is.   There is a string of negatives which we find in three passages in the New Testament which clearly demonstrates that the cause of election is not in man, but in God alone.   *Election is not a natural blessing.*   "*Not of blood*" (John i. 13), is the Divine word in speaking of those who are begotten of the Holy Spirit, and thus become the children of God; and they are begotten because they are elected. Grace does not run in the blood.   As soon might we expect a bird to change itself into a beast, or an olive tree to bear grapes, as expect the natural man to translate himself into the spiritual realm, or any one to transmit spiritual blessings by natural means. *Election is not obtained by the power of man's will.* "*Nor* of the will of the flesh;" "*Not* of him that willeth" (John i. 13; Rom. ix. 16). A hypnotist may by power of will make a pliant subject do as he lists; but no man can by his force of intellect influence God, and cause Him to single out some one person as the object of His mercy and desire. *Election is not because of man's efforts and works.* "*Not* of him that runneth;" "*Not* of works" (Rom. ix. 16; Eph. ii. 9). No more than the men of Babel could bring God to do as they would, because of their colossal effort in the erection of their tower, can man by his labours secure the Divine favour. Salvation is of the Lord; grace is of God; mercy is from above; election is God's choice of those whom He wills. He selects and marks out those who are to be His. What God said to Israel, He says to His people now: "The Lord did not set His love upon you, nor choose you, because ye were more in number than any people; for ye were the fewest of all people; but because the Lord loved you" (Deut. vii. 7, 8). The reason of His choice was in Himself, not in them.

We may find an illustration of God's electing grace in His providence, as Eadie says, "One is born in Europe with a fair face, and becomes enlightened and happy; another is born in Africa with a sable countenance, and is doomed to slavery and wretchedness. One has his birth from Christian parents, and is trained in virtue from his earliest years; another has but a heritage of shame from his father, and the shadow of the gallows looms over his cradle.   One is an heir of genius; another, with some malformation of brain, is an idiot.   Some, under the enjoyment of Christian privilege, live and die unimpressed; others, with scanty opportunities, believe, and grow eminent in piety."

No one who receives the Bible as the revelation of God can question for one moment the sovereignty of God in election, for the Word of God is full of it from Genesis to Revelation.   Seth instead of Cain, Arphaxad instead of Elam, Shem instead of Japheth, Isaac instead of Ishmael, Joseph instead of Reuben, royalty in the fourth son of Jacob, priesthood in the third, and Ephraim instead of Manasseh, are all witnesses of the sovereign elective purposes of God. Yet God never acts in an arbitrary manner, nor does He do anything inconsistent with His character as a merciful and loving God.   "He has the best of reasons for His procedure, though He does not choose to disclose them to us."   Now men of the world often get angry when we preach in this manner, and professing Christians also murmur at the preacher. If the former class will read Luke iv. 25-29, and the latter John vi. 37-66, they will find that it was the same in the days of Christ.   It may simplify the matter if we say that God elects to save one class of people in one way, and if men elect to be saved as God wills it is evidence that they belong to the elect.

God elects to save one class of people.   The class is, those who feel their need of the grace of God.

The sinner feels his need of grace, the foolish one his want of wisdom, the weak their lack of strength, the base their requirement of respectability, and the poor their insufficiency. It is these characters that God meets with His favour (Matt. ix. 13; 1 Cor. i. 27, 28; James ii. 5). It is said that an Arminian being about to pay a Calvinist a sum of money, asked, "Is it decreed that I should pay thee this money?" "Put it in my hand and I will tell thee," was the reply. It would be well that men would see if they are in the conditions that the elect ones are said to fulfil: and the first is, to feel the need of Christ, for this is "the Spirit's rising beam." As the morning light breaking upon the horizon indicates the approach of day, so the convicting of the Spirit in discovering to us our need of the grace of God is proof of the Divine working and favour.

God elects to save in one way. Those who are elected are said to be "chosen in Christ," and "chosen in the Lord" (Eph. i. 4; Rom. xvi. 13). "Chosen in Christ." What does this mean? It signifies that we are *saved in Him*, as the children of Israel were saved, on the night of the Passover, in the passing by of the Lord in judgment, because they were in the blood-sprinkled houses; it speaks of *security in Him*, as Noah and all in the ark were secure from the avenging flood, because God had shut them in; it declares that we are *sanctified in Him*, as the children of Israel were holy to the Lord, because they were represented in their high priest, who had upon his mitre, engraven upon a golden plate, the words, "Holiness to the Lord," that they might always be accepted before Jehovah ; and it tells us that we are *supplied in Him*, as the priests were privileged to feed upon the shew bread, because they were in the priesthood.

The Apostle Paul uses a similar expression in speaking of Rufus, who was "chosen in the Lord" (Rom. xvi. 13). Let us put these two phrases together—"In Christ," and "In the Lord." The first speaks of the *resources* of the believer, whether it be for salvation, Christian life, or service ; and the second declares our *responsibility*, consequent upon the privilege of being "in the Lord." The fact of our being chosen in the Lord Christ Jesus simply means that we are in the line of God's purpose as to His method of salvation, for He will not save in any other way but by being in Christ.

II. THE CONSEQUENCE OF GOD'S ELECTION IS SEEN BY BELIEVERS IN CHRIST.—Archbishop Leighton has well said, in speaking of faith's recognition of God's electing grace, "Though the mariner sees not the pole star, yet the needle of the compass, which points to it, tells him which way he sails. Thus the heart that is touched with the loadstone of Divine love, trembling with godly fear, and yet still looking towards God by fixed believing, points at the love of election, and tells the soul that its course is heavenward, towards the haven of eternal rest."

There is a twofold consequence that is comprehended as we meditate upon the result of God's election.

1. *Apprehending the purpose for which we are chosen.* "Chosen in Him, before the foundation of

the world, that we should be holy, and without
blemish before Him in love" (Eph. i. 4, R.V.). These
words undoubtedly refer to the believer's standing in
Christ as accepted in the holiness and spotlessness of
the Beloved. Yet we cannot separate the practical
from the positional; the former flows out of the
latter, as the rays of light from the sun. An illustration may be found in the nation of Israel, who
were called "a holy people" (Deut. vii. 6), and because they were holy they were to be holy people in
all their actions (Deut. xiv. 2, 21). In like manner
those whom God has chosen in Christ are a holy
nation, and because they are sanctified in Christ they
are to be saintly in life (1 Peter ii. 9; i. 15). The
purpose of His choice is conformity to Him who is
holy. "God elected us as well to the means as to
the end, for as they in Acts xxvii. 31 could not come
safe to land if any left the ship, so neither can men
come to heaven but by holiness." "The Bible never
speaks of men as elected to be saved from the shipwreck, but only as elected to tighten the ropes, and
hoist the sails, and stand at the rudder. Let a man
examine faithfully; let him see that when Scripture
describes Christians as elected, it is as elected to
faith, as elected to sanctification, as elected to obedience: and the doctrine of election will be nothing
but a stimulus to effort." Thus to lay hold of the
purpose God had in view in marking us out as His
own was that we should acknowledge, by our holy
behaviour, that we were the choice of His grace, and
thus, as elect ones, carry out His commands (Col.
iii. 12).

2. *Assuring ourselves that we are elect by making our election sure in adding to our faith what the Lord enjoins.* The Divine exhortation is, " Make your calling and election sure " (2 Peter i. 10). How can we make it sure ?   If the previous verses of 2 Peter i. are noted, it will be seen that it is by supplying to our faith, virtue, knowledge, self-control (*margin*), patience, godliness, and love (2 Peter i. 5-7, R.V.). As the many stones in the building go to make it complete, so these many virtues produce a perfect Christian character.   Or, as the food we eat contains the different constituents of which the body is formed, and goes to build it up and make it strong, so as we minister to our faith the different graces mentioned, we bring about that healthy condition of spiritual life which is an assuring token of our election.

The cause of God's election is His love for us, and the consequence of it is our love to Him.

"Knowing, brethren beloved of God, your election, because (*see margin*) our Gospel came not unto you in word only, but also in power, and in the Holy Ghost, and in much assurance; even as ye know what manner of men we showed ourselves toward you for your sake" (**1 Thess. 1:4,5 R.V.**)

6

MATTER—MANNER—MEN

THERE are two ways in which the usefulness of a life-saving apparatus; as used by the coastguardsmen on our coasts, may be proved. Its use may be explained in a lecture upon its construction, and at once its utility is apprehended in the minds of the hearers; and its beneficent purpose may be exhibited as it is seen at work in a storm, bringing the people from the stranded vessel to the shore. In like manner there are two methods by which a servant of Christ may know that those, to whom he is sent, are chosen of God. First, in his own consciousness, by the manner in which the Holy Spirit accompanies the Gospel; and, second, in the conduct of those who profess to receive the Christ of the Gospel, in the saintliness of their lives. Thus the Apostles knew that the Christians of Thessalonica were the subjects of Divine favour.

Let us consider the token of election, as apprehended in the consciousness of the preacher, in the manner in which the Gospel message comes. In pondering the words that bring this out, there are three things here suggested: the matter of the message, the manner in which the message came, and the men who brought the message.

I. THE MATTER OF THE MESSAGE.—"Our Gospel." It was not some vague harangue evolved from the muddy depths of their own brains that the Apostles gave, but the message that had been committed to them by God.   What that declaration was, as described in the words " our Gospel," may be clearly apprehended if we turn to Acts xvii. 2, 3.   There we are told that the Apostle went into the synagogue and reasoned with the Jews " out of the Scriptures, opening and alleging, that Christ must needs have suffered, and risen again from the dead ; and that this Jesus, whom I preach, is Christ."   In those words there are three facts, namely, the death, resurrection, and exaltation of Christ.   There is expiation by the death of Christ, for He has by His death given full satisfaction to God on account of sin, because He has borne its penalty ; hence those who are in Him are in safe standing, as the trapper who has fired the grass when the prairie is on fire stands where the flames have been.   The resurrection of Christ is God's receipt in full that His claims have been fully met ; and the exaltation of Christ is God's seal to the delight He finds in Him, as evidenced in His crowning Him with glory and honour, and giving Him to be Head over all things to the Church.   The Gospel is condensed in these facts, as Paul says in writing to the Church at Corinth, " I declare unto you the Gospel .   .   .   .   how that Christ died for our sins according to the Scriptures : and that He was buried, and that He rose again the third day according to the

Scriptures " (1 Cor. xv. 1-4). In these facts Paul
delighted, and he calls them " our Gospel," because he
knew their intrinsic value in his own heart and life,
for he did not preach what he did not know to be
true in his own experience, but, like the man who
knows the beneficent properties of a certain herb, he
could confidently commend the truth to others.

To what may the Gospel be compared ? It is the
solid basis upon which we can build. When in
affliction Bolingbroke exclaimed, " Ah ! I find my
philosophy fail me now." The Gospel according to
science, philanthropy, and philosophy, will fail when
nature is breaking up, when sin is apprehended, when
eternity is viewed, and the day of judgment looms
before the vision. But the Gospel of Jesus Christ
tells of sin taken away, judgment for sin borne, Satan
defeated, and death unstung, and thus affords a solid,
unfailing foundation on which to rest. The Gospel is
the *lever to overturn.* It is not merely better than
that which other teachers bring, but it is altogether
distinct, in that it is alive, and all other systems are
dead. There is much truth in the Vedastic ideas of
God, in the views of Zoroaster about sin, in the
eschatology of Egypt, and in the Greek philosophers'
ideas about the chief good ; but all these lack power
to change the heart. Morality will whitewash the
man, but it will not wash him white. The Gospel
alone is that which meets the need of the sinner, as
Bishop Lavington, when addressing the clergy in a
pastoral charge in the last century, said, " We have
long been attempting to reform the nation by moral
preaching. With what effect ? None. On the

contrary, we have dexterously preached the people into downright infidelity.   We must change our voice; we must preach Christ, and Him crucified; nothing but the Gospel is the power of God unto salvation." The Gospel is the lever to move society from its sins; the iniquitous from their dens of infamy; and the sinner from the course of evil.   The Gospel is the *magnet* to attract.   Plato often confessed that he could not bring the inhabitants of a single village to live according to his rules.   Did Paul make that complaint ?   Listen to what he says as he stands before Agrippa, and tells him of the purpose of the Lord in sending him to the Gentiles with the Gospel, in the very words of the Lord Himself:—" To open their eyes, and to turn them from darkness to light, and from the power of Satan unto God, that they may receive forgiveness of sins, and inheritance among them which are sanctified by faith that is in me " (Acts xxvi. 18).

II. THE MANNER IN WHICH THE MESSAGE CAME. —" Not in word only, but also in power, and in the Holy Ghost, and in much assurance."   There is that in a barrel of gunpowder which has in it all the elements of destructiveness, and only wants the light applied for it to show its power to destroy ; but so long as the match and powder are kept apart there is no damage done.   In like manner there is all that in the Gospel of God's grace that will destroy the work of the enemy, regenerate the sinner, and revolutionize society, yet it needs the fire of the Holy Spirit to make it effective, because, if it comes only in word, it will be like the powder unignited ; but if it comes as it did to those of Thessalonica, then it will accomplish its purpose.

There was a fourfold manner in which the Gospel came, namely—in word, in power, in the Holy Ghost, and in much assurance. There are four words which express the method of its approach—faithfully, firmly, fervently, and fully.

Faithfully. "Not in word only," shows that it came in word, and from Acts xvii. 2 we see that it was out of the Scriptures that the Apostle unfolded the necessity and nature of Christ's sufferings. Now, while the Gospel may be faithfully preached, it may only come in word to many, as in the case of the Jews at Antioch, who had heard the truth, yet spoke against those things (Acts xiii. 45); and yet, again, a preacher may be orthodox in his utterance, and not have the unction of the Spirit. We apprehend the former is meant, although it may include the latter.

Firmly. "In power." This seems to indicate that there was no hesitation or trepidation on the part of those who declared the joyful message, but in the firmness of those who were conscious of their position they spoke. On one occasion an obscure man rose up to address the French Convention. "At the close of his oration Mirabeau, the genius of the French Revolution, turned round to his neighbour and eagerly asked, 'Who is that?' The other, who had been in no way interested in the address, wondered at Mirabeau's curiosity; whereupon the latter said, 'That man will yet act a great part;' and added, on being asked for an explanation, 'He speaks as one who believes every word he says.'" They make others feel who feel themselves. " Ye shall be endued with power," was the promise of the Saviour to His timid and trembling disciples.   The power promised was evidently the courage to openly, plainly, and boldly make known the Gospel, as is clearly brought out again and again in the Acts of the Apostles. The boldness and power of utterance of the speakers impressed the council as they looked upon and listened to Peter and John (Acts iv. 13); and of Paul at Rome it is said, that he was " teaching the things concerning the Lord Jesus Christ with all boldness, none forbidding him " (Acts xxviii. 31, R.V.).   See also Acts iv. 29-31; ix. 27-29; xiii. 46; xiv. 3; xviii. 26; xix. 8.   This is what we understand by the Gospel coming in power.

Fervently. " In the Holy Ghost."   The Holy Spirit is the Divine electricity that causes the being to move in holy earnestness of manner.   The Spirit of God is the vital spark that causes the words to come as firebrands, and burn up the conceit of the natural man.   God the Spirit is the Divine Breath who breathes upon the valley of dry bones, and causes them to live in the power of an endless life.   The Eternal Spirit is He who moves upon the chaos and darkness caused by sin, and brings order and light where before there were confusion and emptiness, as He did on the natural world at the beginning.   The Spirit of Truth is the lightning that strikes the sinner with conviction, and causes him to be in terror on account of his iniquity.   The Spirit of Revelation is He that is the eye-salve to remove the blindness of heart, and to unveil to the sinner, in the light of the

holiness of God, the exceeding sinfulness of the sin
that dwells in his nature. The Spirit of Power is He
that draws the unsaved to the Lamb of God, to find
in Him the Remover of guilt. All this, and a good
deal more, is comprehended in the Gospel coming
" in the Holy Ghost."

Fully. " In much assurance." The word " assurance " occurs in three other places, and is rendered
" full assurance." *"Full assurance of understanding"* (Col. ii. 2), or, as the margin of the Revised
Version, " Fulness of understanding." *"Full assurance of hope "* (Heb. vi. 11), or, as the R.V., " Fulness
of hope." *" Full assurance of faith "* (Heb. x. 22),
or, as the R.V., " Fulness of faith." The term " plero-
phoria " is from a word that means to fill up, and is
used to signify the hurrying of a ship on her course,
with all her sails spread and filled with wind. So
one filled with full confidence in the truth of the
Gospel is urged to a course of conduct in harmony
with his conviction. The Apostles had the fullest
confidence in the truth of the Gospel, for they had
proved its power. As Denney says, " They " (the
truths of the Gospel) " are so great that it needs a
certain greatness to answer to them, a certain boldness
of faith to which even a true Christian may be
momentarily unequal; but while he is unequal, he
cannot do the work of an evangelist. Doubt paralyzes.
God cannot work through a man in whose soul there
are misgivings about the truth. At least, His working will be limited to the sphere of what is certain
for him through whom He works: and if we would
be effective ministers of the Word, we must speak

only what we are sure of, and seek the full assurance of the whole truth."

III. THE MEN WHO BROUGHT THE MESSAGE. "Even as ye know what manner of men we showed ourselves toward you for your sake." From these words, the Apostle seems to say, "There is a mutual knowledge between us. We know that you are chosen by the Lord in the way the Gospel came to you, and the effects it produced in and through you; and ye know our characters as preachers; we did not preach one thing and practise another, but we showed, or God manifested through us in our lives, the reality of the truths we proclaimed with our lips."

How has the Gospel message come to us? In word only, as in the case of the stony-ground hearer? In word and power only, as depicted in the thorny-ground hearer? Or in the Holy Ghost and much assurance, as illustrated in the good-ground hearer? In the first the work is all on the surface; there is no depth. In the second, the man receives the Word; he is fully convinced of its truth, but the love of other things kills it. But in the third there is the ploughing of the Spirit, convicting of sin, and the fulness of the Gospel in its blessings and behests flowing into the being.

REPRODUCTION—
RECEPTION—REFLECTION

" And ye became imitators of us, and of the Lord, having received the Word in much affliction, with joy of the Holy Ghost ; so that ye became an ensample to all that believe in Macedonia and Achaia " **(1 Thess. 1:6,7 R.V.)**

7

REPRODUCTION–RECEPTION– REFLECTION

IT is recorded of the Lord Jesus Christ that on one occasion He entered into a house at a certain place, "and would have no man know it: but He could not be hid" (Mark 7: 24). Although He sought seclusion, He was found out by those who were in need of His help. As Christ could not be hid, because of His wonder-working power, as seen in His miracles, so neither can Christ be concealed in the lives of His people, for where He is it must be known, even as lavender will betray its presence by the perfume that comes from it. The grace of God in the heart is like the super-abundance of sap in the vine, which must show itself in the fruit in the branches. Thus the work of grace was seen in the saints at Thessalonica, for they copied the pattern that was seen in the lives of the Apostles, who were exemplifying the life of Christ.

I. Reproduction of the lives of the Apostles and Christ on the characters of the saints.— "And ye became imitators of us, and of the Lord." We watch the child as it imitates the mother, and we see the reproduction of the parent in the similarity of action. There are certain features about the paintings of some artists which indicate the masters they have copied. The ring of the voice, the mode of expression, and the way of putting things, tell out with no uncertainty where the theological student has studied. As the mother is seen in the child, the master in the pupil, and the professor in the student, so the conduct of the Apostles was reproduced in the lives of the saints at Thessalonica, and theirs again was but the stamp of a greater than the greatest of all characters—even Christ. Let us briefly note the twofold imitation.

The imitation of *the Lord's servants.* "Imitators of us." The life of a good man is a stimulus to similarity of action, whether it be seen in the conduct of the friend known to us, or read in the biography. It is said that the leisure of Cæsar was spent in reading the history of Alexander the Great. Upon one occasion his friends found him bathing the book with tears. In deep concern, they asked him the reason why he wept. The reply was, "Do you think I have not sufficient cause for concern, when Alexander at my age reigned over so many conquered countries, and I have not one glorious achievement to boast?" If Cæsar was fired with a longing to imitate Alexander as he read of his victories, should not we be stirred as we think of the list of noble men who have followed in the steps of Christ? As we ponder the patience of Henry Martyn in Persia, the devotion of David Brainerd among the American Indians, the love of the noble army of martyrs, the self-abnegation of Paul and his fellow-labourers, and a host of others, who by their heroic conduct, consecrated lives, and holy living have left their stamp upon the page of history, we must be influenced to copy them.

The imitation of *the Lord.* "And of the Lord." After all, the good and the great that are seen in men are but the reflection of Him who is better than the best and greater than the greatest, as the sun is greater than the moon, which but reflects its light, and would have no light but for it. Well did Dr. Judson express it when one day his wife was telling him that some newspaper had compared him to one of the Apostles. "I do not want to be like Paul, nor Apollos, nor Cephas, nor any mere man. I want to be like Christ. We have only one perfect Exemplar —only One, who, tempted like as we are in every point, is still without sin. I want to follow Him only, copy His teachings, drink in His spirit, place my feet in His footprints, and measure their shortcomings by these, and these only. Oh, to be more like Christ!" Let us imitate Judson in his imitation of Christ. But to imitate Christ there are two things that are necessary. We must know Christ as our Saviour, and we must be indwelt by Christ as our Sanctifier, for we can only imitate the Christ without by the Christ within. The *Copy* for our imitation is set before us in the Word ; and the *Copier* lives within us by His Spirit, and reproduces the Perfect Pattern in proportion as we let Him work in us to will and to do of His good pleasure.

II. RECEPTION OF THE WORD IN MUCH AFFLICTION AND JOY OF THE HOLY GHOST. "Having received the Word in much affliction, with joy of the Holy Ghost." These sentences are like a series of mountain peaks

rising the one above the other.   They might be called
" The range of faith."   In them we have the act,
object, endurance, joy, and power of faith.   *The act
of faith.*   " Ye *received.*"   As Simeon of old, when he
saw the infant Christ, took Him in his arms and was
glad, so, when the Gospel was preached at Thessalonica, those to whom the Apostle writes gladly
accepted the Saviour of whom the Gospel spoke.
The object of faith.   " Having received *the Word.*"
It was not some opinion, notion, or view that had
been evolved from the brains of the preachers, as
the spider spins its web from itself, but the message
which they had received from God, and, as faithful
ambassadors, they had delivered the same, and it was
received as the Word of God, as we are told in
1 Thess. ii. 13.   And in receiving it as the Word of
God the Thessalonians accepted God the Word, even
the Lord Jesus Christ, who is the Object of faith.
The endurance of faith.   " Having received the Word
in *much affliction.*"   Does the affliction here mean
the internal anguish on account of sin, or external
persecution because of decision for Christ ?   Both
meanings might be applied, but undoubtedly the
latter is intended here, as is evident from the his-
torical account in Acts xvii., where we see that the
result of faith in Christ was persecution.   The word
" affliction " is frequently rendered " tribulation " and
" persecution," and the following instances of its use
will illustrate that faith in Christ brings persecution
from the world.   The word of the Lord is, " In the
world ye shall have tribulation " (John xvi. 33).   The
Apostles told the Christians at Lystra, and other

places, that "we must through much tribulation enter into the kingdom" (Acts xiv. 22). The persecution that the believer meets with is illustrated in the case of the early Christians when they were scattered (Acts xi. 19), and John, when he was banished to the Isle of Patmos (Rev. i. 9). *The joy of faith.* "With joy." The stony hearer receives the Word with joy, but he does not accept tribulation and persecution with joy, for when they come he goes back, like Pliable in the *Pilgrim's Progress,* to his former position; and herein lies the difference between a professor and a believer, for the believer, instead of falling back, rejoices that he is counted worthy to suffer shame for the sake of Christ. Denney gives two illustrations of this in his helpful book on Thessalonians.. "'I never knew,'" said Rutherford, 'by my nine years' preaching, so much of Christ's love as He hath taught me in Aberdeen, by six months' imprisonment.' It is a joy that never fails those who face affliction that they may be true to Christ. Think of the Christian boys in Uganda, in 1885, who were bound alive to a scaffolding and slowly burned to death. The spirit of the martyrs at once entered into these lads, and together they raised their voices and praised Jesus in the fire, singing till their shrivelled tongues refused to form the sound :—

> "'Daily, daily, sing to Jesus,
>   Sing, my soul, His praises due ;
> All He does deserves our praises,
>   And our deep devotion too.
>
> "'For in deep humiliation
>   He for us did live below ;
> Died on Calvary's cross of torture,
>   Rose to save our souls from woe.'

Who can doubt that these three are among the chosen of God ? And who can think of such scenes, and such a spirit, and recall without misgiving the querulous, fretful, aggrieved tone of his own life, when things have not gone with him exactly as he could have wished ? " *The power of faith.* " With joy of *the Holy Ghost.*" Ah! this is the secret of joy in sorrow, calm in trouble, glorying in infirmities, and boasting in tribulation. It is not nature's doings, but God's. The Holy Spirit is with us in our sufferings, as the Son of man was with the three Hebrews in the fiery furnace; hence the cause of joy in the midst of suffering. The more Satan pours upon the believer the waters of persecution, the Holy Spirit counteracts his purpose by ministering the oil of gladness; so that the tribulations become so many opportunities to triumph over the enemy's power.

III. REFLECTION OF THE LORD JESUS TO OTHERS. —" So that ye became an ensample to all that believe in Macedonia and Achaia." The meaning of the word " ensample " is a stamp. Its use in other places may be taken in illustration of its meaning. In John xx. 25 it is rendered "*print*," and refers to what Thomas said about Christ, that he would not believe that He was risen until he fully satisfied himself by seeing in His hands the print of the nails, and putting his finger into the print of the nails. As the nails by which Christ was fastened to the cross would leave their mark, so those who are followers of Christ leave their impress upon others. In Acts vii. 44 the word is translated "*fashion*," or, as the R.V., "*figure*," and is used by Stephen in his address

before the council, in calling attention to the fact
that the plan of the tabernacle was received by
Moses, and that he made it according to what he had
seen in the holy mount. As the tabernacle was the
reproduction of the figure Moses had seen in the
mount, so the believer, as he imitates the perfect
Figure that God has placed before him, demonstrates
that he is after the fashion of Him who is perfect,
and thus becomes a model to others, as Paul says to
Titus, "in all things shewing thyself an ensample of
good works" (Titus ii. 7, R.V.). "Example is like
the press : a thing done is the thought printed; it
may be repeated, it cannot be recalled ; it has gone
forth with a self-propagating power, and may run to
the ends of the earth, and descend from generation to
generation." Who knows the power of a holy life ?
The best Christian evidence is to evidence that we
are Christians, *i.e.*, followers of Christ. The un-
answering argument of the fact that Christ is living
is as the life of Christ is manifest by Him through
us. It was the living example of his mother that
convinced Richard Cecil of the truth of Christianity,
and led him to Christ. One night, as he was lying
upon his bed contemplating the character of his holy
mother, he said, "I see two unquestionable facts.
First, my mother is greatly afflicted in circumstances,
body, and mind ; and I see that she cheerfully bears
up under all by the support she derives from con-
stantly retiring to her closet and her Bible.
Secondly, that she has a secret spring of comfort of
which I know nothing; while I, who give an un-
bounded loose to my appetites, and seek pleasure

by every means, seldom or never find it. If, however, there is any such secret in religion, why may I not attain to it as well as my mother? I will immediately seek it of God." We know the result, in the holy life that followed his decision for Christ. How true the words of Rowland Hill are, "We can do more good by being good than in any other way."

What we have said refers rather to the individual Christian, but it will be noted that the Apostle, in speaking of the saints that formed the Church at Thessalonica, speaks of them in the singular. He said of the Church at Corinth that they were the epistle of Christ (2 Cor. iii. 3) It was the Church, as a whole, which was an ensample to those of the believers in Macedonia and Achaia. Thus by the consistency and consecration of the Church at Thessalonica it became a stimulus to the believers at the above-mentioned places. Let us endeavour by our holiness to stir others to more devotion; by our good works to provoke others to do the same; by our love to stir others to love; by our denial of self urge others to follow our example; by our patient perseverance to influence others to endure; by our compassion for the lost to lead others to seek the perishing; and by our whole Christ-like demeanour to draw others closer to the Saviour, whom we profess to love.

SUBJECT—SOUND—
SATISFACTION

"For from you hath sounded forth the Word of the Lord, not only in Macedonia and Achaia, but in every place your faith to God-ward is gone forth ; so that we need not to speak anything" (1 Thess. 1:8 R.V.)

8
SUBJECT—SOUND—SATISFACTION

THE truths of the Gospel in the Old Testament are like hidden treasure, which have to be sought for to be found; but in the New Testament they are as patent to the spiritual man as the costly jewels in the jeweller's shop window, which can be seen and admired by the passing pedestrian. There is an illustration of the sounding out of the Word in the use that the silver trumpets were put to. These silver trumpets were used to call the assembly of Israel together, to direct them in their movements, to give the alarm when an enemy was near, and on festive and sacrificial occasions (Num. 10:1-10). Thus the sounding of the silver trumpets by the priests would be the voice of the Lord to Israel, and the voice of Israel to the Lord. As the priests were the ones who were to blow with the trumpets, so those who are priests unto God through Christ are now privileged to sound the Word of the Lord and the faith to God-ward in the consistent walk of their lives, and by the consecrated witness of their lips.

I. The subject of the sound.— "For from you

hath sounded forth the Word of the Lord. . . . Your faith to God-ward." It will be observed at a glance that the subject that was sounded out was twofold, namely, "the Word of the Lord," and "faith to God-ward." The first may be said to have reference to the Word and its results as seen by men, in the power it exercised upon believers; and the second, to faith in God as translated in the life.

"*The Word of the Lord.*" There are several titles given to the Gospel, as the Word of the Lord. It is the "Word of the Gospel" (Acts xv. 7), for it is the glad tidings that tell out that Christ has died to redeem us, and is raised and accepted for us: it is the "Word of God's grace" (Acts xx. 32), for it is God's loving voice telling us that He extends His favour towards the undeserving; it is the "Word of reconciliation" (2 Cor. v. 19), for it tells us the way is clear for us to come to God, although guilty and condemned; it is the "Word of truth" (2 Cor. vi. 7), for it is God's unerring utterance, upon which we may surely build; it is the "Word of life" (Philip. ii. 16), for it declares Him who alone can communicate spiritual life; it is the "Word of Christ" (Col. iii. 16), for it is that which reveals the person, the offices, and work of our Lord; it is the "Word of righteousness" (Heb. v. 13), for justness is its characteristic, and uprightness is the outcome of belief in it; it is the "Word of faith" (Rom. x. 8), for it tells of a solid foundation on which we can rest; it is the "Word of prophecy" (2 Peter i. 19), for it reveals things to come; it is the "Word of God" (Rom. x. 17), for it commands our obedience; and it is the "Word of the

Lord," as relating to our Lord and Master, Jesus Christ.

As the leaves of a particular tree have a general likeness, yet each leaf may have a peculiar feature, so each of the names of the Gospel has one general characteristic, and yet many shades of meaning, in the one leading thought. This is illustrated in the term "The Word of the Lord." The Word of the Lord is *authoritative*, as may be seen in Acts xiii. 46-49 and 1 Thess. iv. 15. The true servant of Christ has not some view to give or opinion to express, but a message to deliver, which he dare not add to nor take from. The Word of the Lord is *abiding* (1 Peter i. 25), and abiding in the form in which it was uttered, for God is not like some authors who express the same things in different words in subsequent editions of their works. As the molecules of matter are indestructible and therefore abiding, so every utterance of the Lord is eternal and unalterable. The Word of the Lord is *assuring*. It was that Word that Paul and Silas ministered to the jailor's wounded heart, which acted as a balm to a wound, to soothe and satisfy him in his anxiety (Acts xvi. 32). The Word of the Lord is *aggressive*. It assails the enemy of truth, and overturns his defences, and uses those who were opposed to it to become its propagators, as at Ephesus, where, after the truth was preached and accepted, those who had come under its influence confessed their faith in it by burning their heathen and superstitious books (Acts xix. 19).

"*Faith to God-ward.*" This expression, if read in the light of other Scriptures where the words "to

God-ward " occur, seems to indicate a right state of heart and life consequent upon faith in God (see Acts xxiv. 16 ; 2 Cor. iii. 4 ; Philemon 5 ; 1 John iii. 21). As the bitten Israelites in the wilderness looked to the uplifted brazen serpent, and in doing so looked to God for life, so as we look to Christ and trust in His finished work we have faith toward God. As the children of Israel in their journeyings had to look towards the cloudy pillar for guidance, and as it moved they followed, so as we look to the Word and follow its teachings we have faith to God-ward. As Abraham of old, when the Lord called him to leave his own country and follow Him, showed his trust in his obedience, so we evidence our faith toward God as we obey the commands of His truth. As Moses showed his faith towards God in leaving Egypt's sins and pleasures, so the believer proclaims his faith as he turns his face from the Egypt of worldliness and follows the Lord.

II. THE SOUND OF THE SUBJECT.—" From you sounded forth the Word of the Lord, . . . your faith to God-ward is gone forth." The sound spoken of is an image of a trumpet filling with its clear-sounding echo all the surrounding places. Those who have travelled by the coach in the Lake district from Keswick to Ambleside will remember that there is one point in the journey, opposite a well-known mountain, where the guard blows his horn, and after he has done so the hill sends the echo back, and the effect is most thrilling. In like manner the change in the life of the saints was so evident in their turning to God from idols, from unbelief to faith, from hatred to love, from unrest in sin to waiting for Christ from heaven, that it was as the clear, ringing blast of a trumpet, whose sound echoed and re-echoed again.

How may the Word of the Lord be sounded out by us, as a clear, ringing trumpet blast ?

1. *The Word must be trusted in fully with the heart.*   Unless the truth of God impregnates the whole being, as the water fills the sponge, and thus becomes part of our nature, it. will have no influence upon us and others.   If we have any doubt about the Word of the Lord in any part it will be as a parasite that will rob us of our strength and saintliness.   We must be absolutely under its power, fully persuaded of its Divinity, and must unquestioningly accept its conclusions, and faithfully follow its behests ; then its presence will be made known through us, for " when the truth has free course in a man's nature its sound will come forth spontaneously, as fragrance from a June rose, as heat from the fire, as lustre from a diamond, as music from an Æolian harp."

2. The Word of the Lord is sounded out as it is *translated clearly in the life.*   The British and Foreign Bible Society has been able to translate the Bible into 300 languages and dialects, but there is one translation that the Bible Society cannot make, —the translation of the Word of God into the life of the believer.   This can only be done as he obeys the Lord fully, and is empowered by the Holy Spirit. Gibbon attributes the success of Christianity in its earlier days to " the pure and austere morals of the Christian."   Let the Christian young man live a pure and noble life in the midst of temptation ; let the

servant maid serve Christ in her service by doing all out of love to Him; let the business man keep along the lines of righteousness in his trade; let the young lady with leisure fill up her time in Christ-like actions; let the parents rule their household well, by firm, kindly actions; and these shall be a power and the very best transcription of the Word. Who can tell the influence for good such lives will exert, as well as leaving the savour of good names behind. As Dr. Chalmers says, " Live for something ! Do good, and leave behind you a monument of virtue that the storm of time can never destroy. Write your name in kindness, love, and mercy on the hearts of the thousands you come in contact with year by year, and you will never be forgotten. Your name, your deeds, will be as legible on the hearts you leave behind as the stars on the brow of evening. Good deeds will shine as the stars of heaven."

3. The Word of the Lord is sounded out as it is *testified faithfully with the lips.* It seems that the Lord has given to His faithful children in this day of departure from the truth among those who profess to be followers of Christ a peculiar opportunity to contend earnestly for the faith once for all delivered to the saints, and to hold fast the form of sound words. The plenary and verbal inspiration of the Bible is being questioned; and it is for us to maintain that it is God's voice—not His thoughts merely—to man, and to maintain that it is inspired because it claims to be so. The nature of man is said to contain some germs of goodness, which if cultivated shall exterminate the seeds of evil; it is for us to

keep to the truth, which declares that no good thing —from God's standpoint—is in the sinner, and that he needs to be born again ere he can see or enter the kingdom of God. We are told that Christ's sufferings were not necessary to secure salvation, but that they were simply a splendid example of heroic devotion which are set before us that their spirit may inspire us to imitation; it is for us to proclaim that without shedding of blood there is no remission. We are told that Christ by becoming man placed Himself under human conditions, so that He did not know any more than any other man, and that hence, when He said, "Moses wrote of Me," He was simply giving expression to what was generally believed among the Jews; it is for us to testify plainly that such utterances are blasphemous, as they take away from the moral and Divine glory of Christ. We are told that the Holy Spirit is a mere influence proceeding from the Father and the Son, as the breath from the body; it is for us to state the personality of the Holy Spirit, in the very words of Christ Himself, as when He said, "*He* shall testify of Me." At every point let us checkmate the enemies of the truth, whether in the guise of professed friends or open opposers, with "Thus saith the Lord."

In passing it is well to notice how far-reaching the testimony of the saints at Thessalonica was. "In every place," their faith had gone forth. Probably Aquila and Priscilla, who had just come from Rome to Corinth, informed Paul that their conversion had reached the metropolis of the world (Acts xviii. 2). The consecrated lives of believers are like the seeds that are blown hither and thither—they spring up and tell their own story.   Who has not heard of the heroic sufferings of the native Christians in Madagascar, of the consistent conduct of the islanders of the New Hebrides, of the devotion of the natives in Uganda, and many similar facts, which are all the outcome of the Gospel of the grace of God ?

III. The satisfaction that came to the servants of God through the sounding out of the word of God.—" So that we need not to speak anything."   The conversation of those saints spoke so eloquently that there was no need for these servants of God to commend them.   " It was a very suggestive saying of Dr. Lyman Beecher that the reason why he was so blessed to the conversion of men was, that he had so many pulpit reflectors, who lived out and diffused everywhere the Gospel."   If the saints of God will only live out the precepts and principles of the Gospel these will be greater than the greatest evidences ever brought forward.   For, after all, the best proof is the living argument that is seen in the holy and devoted life of one who professes to be a believer in Christ.   And what joy and satisfaction such minister to those who are responsible for guiding the flock of God !   Trapp has well said, " A good people may ease their pastor of a good deal of pain."

TURNING—SERVING—WAITING

" For they themselves report concerning us what manner of entering in we had unto you ; and how ye turned unto God from idols, to serve a living and true God, and to wait for His Son from heaven " (1 Thess. 1:9,10 R.V.)

9

TURNING—SERVING—WAITING

IT was the writer's privilege some years ago to conduct a series of special evangelistic meetings, in a number of villages in the heart of England, extending over a period of three or four months. There were many who professed to turn to the Lord. The work at one place — designated by Shakespeare as "Drunken B———," because he got intoxicated there once — was most marked. The public-houses were emptied, and Satan was roaring like a lion, as he generally does when he loses those who have been under his sway; but the work went on, for the Lord's people were united and prayerful. The news of what the Lord was doing, in breaking down the self-righteous and lifting up the profligate, spread right and left, like a prairie fire. Soon believers came from the surrounding villages, and when they saw what changes God had wrought in the lives of many, they bore testimony to the working of the Holy Spirit through His servant; hence they showed to others what manner of entrance the evangelist had in the way the Gospel came, and was received and reflected by those who accepted it.

The experience of Paul and his fellow-labourers

was the same. The report about them was that they had come to Thessalonica and preached about Christ with such energy and emphasis that none could gainsay their message; and, more than that, many of the citizens had not only given credence to the words of these strange messengers, but they had been converted, as was evident in their turning to God from idols, and in the attitude they maintained in serving Him, and waiting for His Son from heaven. There is no need to repeat the words that describe the manner in which the Gospel came, as stated in verse 5. We draw attention to the manifestation of the power of the Gospel as illustrated in the lives of those to whom the Epistle was written. The three words that head this Bible reading mark the ascent in their upward course.

I. Turning.—" Ye turned unto God from idols." Apostasy, idolatry, conversion, and separation are all found in the words, " Ye turned," &c. Man has left God, as the prodigal left his father's house, and gone off into the land of self-will and sin, and by doing so he has placed himself under Satanic power and authority; but Satan is a wise slaveholder, and to get the greater hold upon those who have come into his domain he seeks to get them occupied with some object which shall attract and captivate, as the glittering and beautifully spotted snake casts a spell over its victim to destruction. There are many idols that are being worshipped, beside those of wood and stone. There are many who pity the heathen idol worshipper, who have greater need to pity themselves. How many there are who bow to the golden calf,

although they worship it in a more portable way than
the children of Israel! The "almighty dollar" is the
only almighty to many. Righteousness, truth,
honesty, and compassion are sacrificed at Mammon's
shrine. There are thousands who prostrate themselves before the god Bacchus. Virtue, honour, love,
and every good and noble thing are ground beneath
its car. Many prostrate themselves before the god-
dess of unchastity, and are her helpless slaves. Others
bow to the god of ceremony. Lifeless forms, bowings,
eastward position, priestism, chantings, almsgiving,
saints, and a hundred and one things are put in the
place of Christ. Now, when the Gospel comes in
power, it revolutionizes the whole of the man.
Reformation is not sufficient. The Dagons of idolatry
must fall before the ark of God, and be not only broken,
but expelled and abandoned. It is said that one of
the missionaries of the China Inland Mission was the
means of a large Chinese heathen temple being
turned into a Christian place of worship. "The
temple looks very pleasant in its changed character.
The two large bells now call the people to worship
the living God, instead of calling the idol, as they
supposed, from his feasts and slumbers. In the front
temple quaint pictures of flying spirits and genii,
painted on the walls, still remain. The large temple
makes a very neat mission chapel, with its whitened
walls and scarlet-painted posts and beams. The
wooden incense table has been cut down into a
preaching table, and the benches are made from the
platform which supported the larger idols. On the
temple front hangs a large tablet, with 'Jesus'

Chapel' in beautiful Chinese characters, replacing the old Taonist sign. This temple now stands a distinct witness to the truth that God is a Spirit, and His glorious Gospel is proclaimed in it." The change is as distinct in the life of him who believes in the Lord Jesus Christ as the transformation in the temple in China.

"Unto God." These words give us the key to the secret of the change, for to turn to God is to be saved and kept by Omnipotence. Unto the God of grace, from the idol of self-righteousness; unto the God of truth, from the lies of Satan's making; unto the God of love, from the hatred begotten by sin; unto the God of power, from the weakness of self-effort; unto God the Father, to be His children, and obey His commands, from being the children of the wicked one; unto God the Son, to be united to Him as the branch is to the vine, thus turned from the hostile position of an unbeliever; and unto God, the Holy Spirit, to be sealed and sanctified, hence turned from the position of enmity and sin. And mark the distinctiveness of their conversion. It was not a gradual turning, but a clear and unmistakable action. As distinct as when the steamer is going west and is turned about and goes east. "Ye turned," &c., and in turning they were separated to God, and the old manner of life was left, as when one discards a suit of clothes. How is this attitude to be maintained? By continual faith in God our Saviour, by unceasing prayer to God our Father, and by being always under the direction of God our Comforter.

II. SERVING.—"To serve a living and true God."

The One who is served, and those who serve, are here made known.

1. *The One who is served.* "Living and true God." He is the living and true God, in contrast to the dead idols. They have eyes, but they see not; ears, but they hear not; lips, but they speak not; and hands, but they aid not. *The living God has eyes to behold.* He sees to search the evil in His people, as He is represented in the Revelation when John saw Him with eyes as flames of fire searching the evil in the seven Churches of Asia. He comes to discover the evil of worldliness, the baseness of selfishness, the canker of covetousness, the mixed motive, the lack of stability in the faith, and the want of love. But those eyes are not only as flames of fire to discover evil, but they are also as the eyes of doves (S.S., v. 12)—tender and loving, watching over us to befriend us, so that when He sees us in danger He may come to our aid, as when Christ saw His disciples toiling in rowing, and came to them and brought them safe to land (Mark vi. 48). *The living God has ears to hear.* "Call upon Me, . . . and I will hearken" (Jer. xxix. 12): "Call upon Me, and I will answer" (Jer. xxxiii. 3): "Call upon Me . . . I will deliver" (Psalm l. 15), are His gracious assurances, and we never call in vain, for He is always more than true to His promise. *The living God has hands to help.* The comforting trinity of promise in Isaiah xli. 10 comes stealing into the spirit as the fresh perfume of the sweet-briar on the summer breeze. He says, "Weak one, 'I will strengthen thee;' sinking one, 'I will uphold thee;' and desponding one, 'I will help

thee.'" *The living God has lips to speak.* He speaks in accents of love to welcome and to warn. He welcomes us to the throne of grace with the unlimited promise of "Whatsoever ye shall ask in My name, that will I do" (John xiv. 13); and He reminds us that "Whatsoever we do, we should do all for the glory of God" (1 Cor. x. 31).

Now the One whom we serve is not only said to be "living," but also "true." He is the "true God" in contrast to the false gods—idols. They were lies, deceptions, the product of man's corrupt mind, and the standing evidence of his apostasy from God. In contrast to the shams of men stands the Eternal Verity, who is the great "I AM." The self-existing, ever-present, unchanging, eternal One.

2. *Those who serve.* Those who are turned to God, and those alone, are they who are called to serve God. What are the lines upon which service to God runs? *The cross is its birth-place and starting point.* We are saved to serve, we do not serve to be saved. The life is a blank till we know Christ as our Saviour in the sight of God. As Israel were a people to worship and serve God from the time that they left the blood-sprinkled houses in Egypt, but not before, so when we accept Christ as our Paschal Lamb to shield from wrath we begin to serve—but not before, for all God's servants must have the blood mark of redemption upon them.

The Bible is the authority and rule in service. The servant of God is not an agent who carries on business apart from the Lord, nor a partner who can express his own views, but a servant who is responsible to obey. "Thus saith the Lord" is his authority, and he has no authority save as he is under the authority of Christ. The Scriptures are his rule, and every action must square to them, for it to be right. As Moses did "as the Lord commanded" without any subtraction or addition, so will every true servant.

All things are in the scope and sphere of Christian service. As in the coming day of Christ's millennial glory " Holiness to the Lord " shall be upon the bells of the horses, and every pot in Jerusalem (Zech. xiv. 20, 21), so whatever may be the sphere in which we move, and whatever we may have to do, be it the duties of the home, the work of the shop, the business of the counter, the menial service, the common round —it should be done as serving the Lord Christ.

The glory of God is the aim and end of Christian service. As the runner in the race keeps his eye on the goal, and puts forth all his power to reach it, so the true servant seeks in all things to please his Lord, and thus to glorify Him. The highest ambition of every servant of Christ is to be able to say to God in his measure as his Master, " I have glorified Thee on the earth; I have finished the work which Thou gavest me to do " (John xvii. 4; 2 Tim. iv. 7).

Christ is the Pattern and Lord of Christian service. What Christ was, what He did, how He acted—is the Perfect Copy that is set before us for our imitation. He bids us look to Him, as Gideon said to his men, "Look on me, and do likewise . . . as I do, so shall ye do" (Judges vii. 17).

The Holy Spirit is the Power and Inspiration in

Christian service. The Lord not only bids us do, but He bestows the power. The only thing for us to remember is, that we have to obey the condition through which the strength of God flows to us, for as the wheel of the water mill is only moved as the water flows over it, and hence for the supply to be diverted means a cessation of the power, so as we are responsive to the Divine conditions, the Holy Spirit works unhindered through us.

The judgment seat of Christ is the place of test and reward for service. The motives that have actuated us, and the quality of our work, will then be revealed, and our reward will be according to faithfulness in our stewardship.

III. WAITING.—"To wait for His Son from heaven." Waiting for Christ is "the bloom of Christian character." If we are not waiting for Christ there is a great want in the life, and it is a clear indication that the hand of the world or ignorance has taken the bloom off our Christian character. "Death is the coming of Christ," so say some. If those who believe this will prayerfully read the last chapter of John's Gospel, it will there be seen that Christ distinguishes between death and His coming. Christ had been telling Peter that he would die, and Peter clearly apprehends this, as he says in his Second Epistle (2 Peter i. 14). Now Peter was anxious to know what John was to do, but Christ says, "If I will that he tarry till I come, what is that to thee ? follow thou Me. This saying therefore went forth among the brethren that that disciple should not die." From these words it will be seen at once that the Lord dis-

tinguished and the disciples apprehended the difference between His coming and death. Others say that
"the Lord came when the Holy Spirit was given."
But the Lord speaks of *"Another* Comforter" in
referring to the coming of the Holy Spirit, and how
can such words describe His own coming? Impossible!
As the Scriptures which have reference to Christ's
coming in humiliation were literally and personally
fulfilled, so those which designate His second coming
will be likewise.

The Person whom we expect. "His Son." Here
we are reminded that Christ is not only Divine, but
that He is Deity, namely, one with God in every
sense of the word. Not to accept the Son as the
Eternal Son of God is to reject the Father (1 John
ii. 23), and to be void of eternal life (1 John v. 12).
The eternal Sonship of Christ is the foundation of
our salvation (Acts viii. 37), and the keystone to the
arch of truth. Limit or take this away, and we have
no basis for the one, nor stability for the other.
His Son! The Holy Spirit loves to play upon these
words. We hear their music again and again in the
Word, and they thrill through our spirits with joy
and satisfaction. The importance and inspiration of
this truth will be seen at once if the Scriptures,
where the words "His Son"* occur, are pondered.

---

* (1) The Scriptures speak concerning "His Son" (Rom. i. 3). (2)
God sent His Son to speak (Heb. i. 2); He was His gift (John iii. 16);
He sent Him to save (John iii. 18); to judge sin in Him (Rom. viii. 3);
He was the expression of His love and righteousness (Rom. viii. 32);
He sent Him to redeem (Gal. iv. 4, 5); He sent Him to be the Propitia-
tion for our sins (1 John iv. 10); and that we might have life through
Him (1 John iv. 9). (3) The Father's testimony about Him must be
believed (1 John v. 9, 11). (4) He is the One who is revealed to, and in,

There are many characters in which Christ will appear when He comes again for His own. He comes as the *Gatherer* for His people; He comes as the *Saviour* to complete our salvation; He comes as the *Bridegroom* for His bride; He comes as the *Lord* to reward His servants; He comes as the *Bright and Morning Star* to gladden our hearts; He comes as our *Hope* to fulfil His promise; and He comes as the *Son* to reap the reward of His anguish and atonement on the cross. Then shall be fulfilled the prophecy, " He shall see of the travail of His soul, and be satisfied."

The place from whence He will come. " From heaven," or more correctly, " The heavens." The word is in the plural. The word " heaven" is used in one of three senses in the Scriptures. Perhaps the words " air" (Matt. vi. 26), " sky " (Matt. xvi. 2), and " heaven," best express the difference. The first tells us that it is the place where the birds fly; the second, that it is the firmament; and the third that it is the dwelling-place of God (Acts vii. 49). Christ was seen to go into heaven by those who were His followers, and they were told that He would come in like manner as they had seen Him go away (Acts i. 10, 11). Stephen also saw Him in the heavens, at the right hand of God. He with the eagle eye of faith saw the Son of God waiting to receive him to Himself

---

the believer (Gal. i. 16). (5) God gives the Spirit of His Son to those who believe (Gal. iv. 6). (6) He brings those that believe into the kingdom of His Son (Col. i. 13); yea, they are said to be "in Him" (1 John v. 11, 20). (7) We are called to have fellowship with His Son (1 Cor. i. 9 ; 1 John i. 3). (8) And as we walk in the light the blood of His Son cleanseth from all sin (1 John i. 7).

(Acts vii. 56). Christ is said to be there (Mark xvi. 19), and He will be there till the time of His coming again to restore all things (Acts iii. 21, R.V.). He is there as the High Priest who carries on His priestly work on behalf of His people (Heb. iv. 14, vii. 26, viii. 1); and as their Master whom they are to obey, and to whom they are responsible (Ephes. vi. 9). From the heavens He shall come (1 Thess. iv. 16), to receive His own to Himself according to His promise.

The posture in which believers should be found. " *Wait* for His Son," &c. That this is the attitude of believers who are truly alive to their Lord's promise we are plainly told again and again. We are waiting for Christ to complete our salvation. As He died once to free us from the punishment due to our sin by bearing it for us, and as He lives to keep us from the power of sin by the indwelling of the Holy Spirit, so shall He appear a second time, apart from sin, to them that wait for Him unto salvation (Heb. ix. 28, R.V.), for then He shall save us from the presence of sin, as Paul says in writing to the Church at Rome: " Waiting for our adoption, to wit, the redemption of our body " (Rom. viii. 23, R.V.). The Apostle gives expression to the same in writing to the saints at Philippi, " We wait for a Saviour, the Lord Jesus Christ, who shall fashion anew the body of our humiliation, that it may be conformed to His body of glory " (Philip. iii. 20, 21, R.V.). "A servant of Christ once entered an ancient almshouse, of which an aged couple were the inmates. Beside a little round table, opposite the fire, sat the husband, too paralyzed to move at his entrance, and with his hat on his head to keep off the gusts of wind which sifted through his chinky dwelling. His wooden shoe pattered on the floor unceasingly, keeping time to the tremor of his shaking frame; and, as he was deaf, his visitor shouted in his ear, ' Well, what are you doing ? ' ' Waiting, sir.' ' For what ? ' ' For the appearing of my Lord.' ' And what makes you wish for His appearing ? ' ' Because I expect great things then. He has promised a crown of righteousness to all them that love His appearing.' " As the aged pilgrim was waiting for his Lord, so every believer should be found in this attitude of expectancy.

But, further, what should be the characteristics of our waiting ?

We should wait with *watchful eye.* " Ye yourselves be like unto men that wait for their Lord, when He will return from the wedding; that, when He cometh and knocketh, they may open unto Him immediately. Blessed are those whom the Lord, when He cometh, shall find watching. Verily I say unto you that He shall gird Himself, and make them to sit down to meat, and will come forth and serve them. And if He shall come in the second watch, or come in the third watch, and find them so, blessed are those servants " (Luke xii. 36-38). The form of the parable is Eastern. It pictures a lord who has gone to the wedding of a friend. The festivities would spread over many days, so that the servants would not know when he would return; but they were responsible to be on the look out for him, and be ready to greet him when he came. Our Lord has gone to His Father's right hand, and bids us wait for

Him with watchful eye, so that His coming shall not be a surprise to us. As aged Simeon, Anna, and many others were "waiting for the consolation of Israel" (Luke ii. 25, 38) at Christ's first coming, so we should be waiting for Him who is coming again.

We should wait with *girded loins*. "Let your loins be girded" (Luke xii. 35). "Gird up the loins of your mind; be sober, and hope to the end for the grace that is brought unto you at the revelation of Jesus Christ" (1 Peter i. 13). "Your loins girt about with truth" (Ephes. vi. 14). The loins being girded indicates preparedness for service, as we have it illustrated in the action of the Lord Jesus when about to wash His disciples' feet (John xiii. 4). Taking the above Scriptures and the illustration, and putting them together, the meaning undoubtedly is, the truth of God is the girdle to strengthen our minds to serve the Lord continually and faithfully till He comes. This is an image from the Israelites eating the Passover with the loose outer robe girded up about the waist with a girdle as for a journey. Workmen, pilgrims, runners, wrestlers, and warriors so gird themselves up, both to prevent the garment impeding motion, and to brace up the body for action. The believer is to have his mind collected, and always ready for Christ's coming.

We should wait with *trimmed and burning lamps.* " Your lights burning" (Luke xii. 35). " Looking for the blessed hope and appearing . . . of our great God and Saviour Jesus Christ" (Titus ii. 13, R.V.). The burning lamp is indicative of a clear and faithful witness, consequent upon a holy life. Christ said of

John the Baptist that he " was a burning and a shin-ing light " (John v. 35).   As to character, there was not a greater than he ; hence his testimony to Christ was so effective.   For the lamp of our life to be right, it must be trimmed with holiness of conduct and prayerful devotion to Christ, so that the snuffs of selfishness and worldliness may be kept away ; and our life must be fed with the oil of the Spirit's grace that we burn with whole-hearted love to Christ and men, " so that we come behind in no gift ; waiting for the coming of our Lord Jesus Christ " (1 Cor. i. 7).

We should wait with *pure heart.*   "We shall see Him even as He is.   And every one that hath this hope set on Him purifieth himself, even as He is pure " (1 John iii. 2, 3, R.V.).   A pure heart is a heart possessed by Christ.   The unclean birds may come upon the sacrifice of our being, but in the name of Christ we shall drive them away, as Abraham drove away the fowls that would light upon his offerings (Gen. xv. 11).   When Christ comes into the heart He drives out all that is contrary to His will, as He did the desecrators of the Temple when He was upon earth. Now those who are looking for Christ seek to be as Christ here, in that they purify themselves from all filthiness of the flesh and spirit, and " perfect holiness in the fear of God."

THE SUPERLATIVENESS
OF DIVINE THINGS

"And to wait for His Son from heaven, whom He raised from the dead, even Jesus, which delivereth us from the wrath to come" (1 Thess. 1:10 R.V.)

10
THE SUPERLATIVENESS
OF DIVINE THINGS

THERE is "multum in parvo" in this verse. There is a mountain of matter in every line, yea, there is a casket of jewels in each word, and it illustrates in a striking way the saying of Tertullian, "I adore the plenitude of the Scriptures, in which every letter is a word, and every word is a verse, and every verse is a chapter, and every chapter is a book, and every book is the Bible; in which every twig is a branch, and every branch a tree, and every tree a forest; in which every drop is a rivulet, and every rivulet a river, and every river a bay, every bay the ocean, every ocean all waters."

Instead of giving a general exposition, we shall note the superlativeness of several subjects mentioned:—

I. CHRIST'S HIGHEST TITLE.—Christ is called "His Son" in speaking of His relative position with the Father. The reference is here made to His eternal Sonship, and not to His acquired Sonship. The eternal Sonship of Christ is the qualification that gave Him the right to act as our Daysman. As the sent One of God, He was great, for He was God's Prophet; as the Sacrifice for sin, He was greater, for He was God's Provision; but as the Son He was greatest, for He was God Potentially, who gave life to His words, and efficacy to His sacrifice; hence the Son of God is God the Son.

It is related that two gentlemen were once disputing on the Deity of Christ. One of them, who argued against it, said, " If it were true it certainly would have been stated in more clear and unequivocal terms."

" Well," said the other, " admitting that you believed it, were you authorized to teach it, and allowed to use your own language, how would you express the doctrine to make it indubitable ?"

" I would say," replied he, " that Jesus Christ is the true God."

" You are very happy," rejoined the other, " in the choice of your words, for you have happened to hit upon the very words of inspiration. John, speaking of the Son, says, ' This is the true God, and eternal life ' " (1 John v. 20).

II. CHRIST'S SWEETEST NAME. — " Jesus." The name of " Lord " is sweet; it is like the ringing sound of the priestly trumpet which commanded Israel to move on in their wilderness march, for it speaks of His sovereignty. The name of " Christ " is sweeter; it is like the abundant supply that came to Israel when the water gushed from the smitten rock, for it makes known to us the supply of His grace, as the Living One; but the name of " Jesus " is sweetest; it is like the sweet-smelling gum that comes from the

pierced myrrh tree. It is because Jesus has been
wounded in death for us that He is "made both
Lord and Christ." He could never have been the
latter had it not been for the former. Besides, the
name Jesus reminds us of His humanity. It is the
key to the whole of revelation, as the old negress
said to the teacher, "Now I want to learn to spell
'Jesus,' for it 'pears to me that the rest will come
easy if I learn to spell that blessed name first."

III. CHRIST'S GREATEST ACCOMPLISHMENT.—Christ
is said in the verse to have died, and by that death
we apprehend that He has accomplished the greatest
work possible. His creative acts were a great work,
when He, by His fiat, caused things to be, as it is
significantly stated in the first chapter of Genesis in
connection with those words "He said." His
miraculous deeds when on earth were greater, as He
healed the sick, cleansed the lepers, released the
demon-possessed, and raised the dead. But the
greatest work of all was when He died upon the cross.
For by the humbling of His death He has overcome
the proud; by the weakness of His death He has
taken the spoil from the strong; by the sufficiency of
His death He has made complete atonement for sin;
by the fact of His death He has been the death of
death; by the value of His death he has purchased
untold blessings; by the power of His death He has
swept away every hindrance that stood in between us
and God; and by the voluntariness of His death He
has glorified God.

IV. GOD'S MIGHTIEST ACT.—"Whom He raised
from the dead." There are three expressions which

may be said to embody all that God is, and hence the ground of all that He does, and these are—

"GOD IS A SPIRIT."

"GOD IS LOVE."

"GOD IS LIGHT."

"God is a Spirit," and as such He is the Source and Sustenance of every living thing.   That mysterious something which we call "life" is from Him who is the Spirit of Life, hence He is the Almighty One; "God is love," and as such He gave His only begotten Son as the expression of His intense desire that all men should be saved; and "God is Light," and as such He raised His Son from the dead, as His Justifier, and as His acknowledgment that He was honoured by the finished work of Him whom He had given for sin and sinners.   The resurrection of Christ is God's answer to any who would bring a charge against the believer in Him (Rom. viii. 34); the resurrection of Christ is God's receipt in full that all claims have been discharged by the death of Christ; and the resurrection of Christ is God's pledge that all who have fallen asleep, and those who remain, who belong to Him, at His coming, shall be for ever with Him; and the Holy Spirit as the seal within the believer is the assurance that it shall surely be.

V. CHRIST'S LOFTIEST PLACE.—Christ has ascended through the heavens to the Father's right hand, and there He sits on His throne with Him.   Christ occupied a lofty place, as the Messenger of the covenant as revealed in the Old Testament, for He was the channel of communication between the seen and the unseen, as illustrated when He came to Abraham and spoke to Him about Sodom. In the New Testament He fills a loftier situation, as the Apostle sent of God to reveal His character and to carry out His will. "My meat is to do the will of Him that sent Me, and to finish His work" (John iv. 34); but Christ now occupies the loftiest position, for He is seen as the Overcomer (Rev. iii. 21), sitting on His father's throne. Hence we apprehend the meaning of the expression, that He is "made higher than the heavens" (Heb. vii. 26).

VI. CHRIST'S STRONGEST WORK.—"Delivereth us from the wrath to come." As the Revised Version brings out, this refers not merely to His past action in redeeming us, but to the present office He fills as the Deliverer. As Christ in His life kept on His steady course, although the hatred of man, the faithlessness of friends, the agony of Gethsemane, and the cruel cross of Calvary stood before Him, as that through which He must pass, He showed that He was strong in the stedfastness of purpose that possessed Him. As He meets with the arch-enemy of God and man—"the strong man armed," who "keepeth his goods in peace"—He manifests that He is stronger than he, in that He defeats and spoils him. But in that He keeps those who trust in Him from the "wrath to come," because He has borne the wrath for them, He declares that He is strongest. There is a present punishment that sin brings, in the shame, remorse, fear, and isolation that are its bitter fruit; and there is also a wrath to come, for the present retribution that often overtakes the sinner is but a harbinger of the future, as the lurid clouds are the forerunners of the coming storm. But the believer being in Christ, it can never touch him, for before it can do so it must touch Christ, and that can never be.

VII. CHRIST'S FULLEST GLORY.—There is a threefold glory which Christ has as the Son of man. There was the full moral glory of His character, which shone out in the holiness of His life like the sun in its strength, as John says, " We beheld His glory, the glory as of the Only Begotten of the Father " (John i. 14); there was the fuller glory which the Father gave Him in consequence of His faithful work, when He " crowned Him with glory and honour " (Heb. ii. 9); but the fullest glory that He shall yet have is when He comes again in the glory of His Father to receive us to Himself, for then His prayer shall be answered—" Father, I will that they whom Thou hast given Me be with Me . . . that they may behold My glory " (John xvii. 24).

VIII. THE BELIEVER'S GRANDEST HONOUR.—" To wait for His Son." It is grand, as poor outcast, lost, undone, rebellious, hell-deserving sinners, to be allowed to believe in Christ unto salvation; it is grander, as believers in Christ, to make known our love to Him by obeying His Word; but the grandest privilege of all is to wait in humble expectancy for that Lord who has promised to come again, for, as Trapp says, " This is pinned as a badge to the sleeve of every believer, that he looketh and longeth for Christ's coming. The old character of God's people

was, they waited for the consolation of Israel—
Christ's first coming; so it is now, the earnest
expectation of His second coming."

Are we patiently waiting for the coming of Christ?
It was the fact of Christ's coming that lived and
glowed in the hearts of the early Christians, and in
that we have the reason for their unworldliness of
life, their intensity of purpose in service for Christ,
their united prayerfulness in waiting upon Christ,
and their holy devotion in consecration to Christ. Is
it because the characteristics of the early disciples
are wanting to a great extent in the lives of professing Christians to-day that the corresponding waiting
for Christ is absent in them?

" The Gospel of God " (1 Thess. 2:2,8,9)

11
THE GOSPEL OF GOD

IF there was one thing more than another that was the absorbing theme of the ministry of the Apostle Paul, it was "the Gospel," for it was to this that he was separated (Rom. 1:1), and that Gospel was what he calls three times over in this chapter "The Gospel of God," namely, the glad tidings which he had received from God. It was not some theory that had been evolved from his own brain, like the spider's web made from its own bowels; it was not some opinion which had been gathered from the statements of others, like that of some who read the utterances of a scientific lecturer, and at once give out the view they have adopted; but it was a message from God which he held as a sacred trust, and which he was responsible to deliver.

What a Gospel to preach! It is Divine in its authority, coming like the word of a king, with power; it is deep in its contents, for there are in it depths which cannot be sounded, heights which cannot be reached, lengths which cannot be measured, and breadths which cannot be comprehended; it is distinct in its utterance, coming like the clear ringing trumpet sound at the year of jubilee, which meant freedom to the slave, and the restoration of the lost inheritance to the Israelite; it is definite in

its offer, coming, like the unmistakable Word of God
through Moses to Israel, when they were told to look
to the brazen serpent for life ; it is *diffusive* in its
influence, coming as the light, bringing life and gladness to the whole being of those who believe in
Christ ; it is *decisive* in its claims, for, while it frees
from the yoke of sin, it places upon its adherents the
yoke of the Saviour ; and it is *durable* in texture, for
it is the strong cable which moors us to the throne
of God. So much for the general characteristics of
the Gospel, but what are its contents ?

There is an eightfold aspect of the Gospel as
follows :—God is its Author ; the death and resurrection of Christ are its axis ; the Spirit of God is its
Applier ; faith in Christ is the means by which it is
apprehended ; holiness of life is its appointment ; the
Person of Christ is its attraction ; love is its atmosphere ; and the coming of Christ is its apex.

I. GOD IS THE AUTHOR OF THE GOSPEL.—The
Gospel is called " The Gospel of *God*."   We admire a
beautiful picture, and we ask, " Who is the artist ? "
We note the proportions of a magnificent building,
and we inquire, " Who is the architect ? "   We take
up a handsome and expensive watch, and we open it
to see who is the maker.   We are given a new book,
and we look to see who is the author.   In like
manner we want to know who is the author of the
Gospel, for as the name of a well-known author commands our attention, so does the Gospel, as we call to
mind that the Gospel is the " Gospel of God."   As
the tabernacle in the wilderness was the conception
of God, as revealed to Moses when he was with Him

in the holy mount, so the glad tidings of God's provision for sinful men originated in God Himself.
How often the Lord Jesus enforces this in His para-
bles! It was the King Himself who prepared the
marriage feast at the nuptials of His Son; and it is
the Father who is represented as watching for the
return of the prodigal. The angels sing to the glory
of God as they make known the glad tidings to the
shepherds, for they know that they were sent by
Him: and Christ speaks of God sending Him, and
loving the world.

II. THE DEATH AND RESURRECTION OF CHRIST
ARE THE AXIS OF THE GOSPEL.—Astronomers tell us
that the cluster of stars known as the Pleiades is the
centre of the universe. The meaning of the Hebrew
word used in Job ix. 9 and xxxviii. 31 seems to imply
this, for it signifies " the hub," or " a heap." As the
group of the Pleiades is supposed to be the hub of
the universe, around which all the rest of the suns
and planets revolve as the spokes of a wheel around
its hub, so the death and resurrection of Christ are
the axis around which all God's dealings with men
turn, and in which all His purposes centre. It is a
most interesting and profitable study to ponder carefully and prayerfully the blessings that come to us
as a refreshing shower to the parched ground, and
the responsibilities that rest upon us as a solemn
charge, in consequence of our faith in the death and
resurrection of Christ. As a united testimony is
given on a proved axiom of science, such as that the
atmosphere is made up of oxygen, nitrogen, &c., so
the witness of the prophets, the voice of the sacrifices,

the utterances of the Apostles, the testimony of John the Baptist, the inspired Word of the Holy Spirit, the teaching of Christ Himself, and the expressions of the Father—all focus and make up one grand long chorus of evidence that the death and resurrection of Christ are the centre of all God's purposes with man, and that all His dealings with men come through the Man at His own right hand.

III. THE SPIRIT OF GOD IS THE APPLIER OF THE GOSPEL.—It was not sufficient for our blue-jackets when they were commissioned to bombard Alexandria to have perfect cannons, dry powder, and adequate shells; neither would the desired result be accomplished supposing the cannon were in position, the powder and shells rammed home—there would still be something wanting. What is it? It is the application of the fuse, which shall ignite the powder, and send the shells on their deadly mission. In like manner there must be the cannon of a consecrated life in the messenger of the Gospel, who must be charged with the powder and shell of the Word of the Gospel; but, after all, it is the Holy Spirit, as the baptism of fire, who must cause the truth to go forth in its fiery, convincing power to the heart of the sinner, that the earthworks which he has erected may be scattered, and that he may surrender to the Lord Jesus in humble confession and in simple faith.

IV. FAITH IN CHRIST IS THE MEANS BY WHICH THE GOSPEL IS APPREHENDED.—It is not sufficient that the words of Christ be accepted as true, nor that the example of Christ be imitated, nor that the life of Christ be admired, nor that an assent be given that the death of Christ is the exhibition of God's love, nor that the resurrection of Christ be accepted as the most stupendous miracle ever performed, but there must be the definite personal faith in Christ. Faith in Christ! What is it? It is the personal belief that Christ died for our sins and rose again for our justification, which leads us to commit ourselves unreservedly to Him, confidently resting in His own word for assurance that we are forgiven and accepted, and a humble trust which expresses itself in a life of dependence upon the Son of God.

V. HOLINESS OF LIFE IS THE APPOINTMENT OF THE GOSPEL.—There have been those who preached *a* Gospel which gives a licence to sin, but *the* Gospel gives no such permission, as those who have not believed in it have confessed. Bolingbroke confessed that " no religion has ever appeared in the world of which the natural tendency is so much directed as the Christian to promote the peace and happiness of mankind ; and the Gospel is one continued lesson of the strictest morality, of justice, charity, and universal benevolence." The testimony of Gibbon is akin : " While the Roman Empire," says he, " was invaded by open violence, or undermined by slow decay, a pure and humble religion greatly insinuated itself into the minds of men, grew up in silence and sobriety, derived new vigour from opposition, and finally erected the banner of the cross on the ruins of the capital." Again, he says, " The Christian religion is a religion which diffuses among the people a pure, benevolent, and universal system of ethics, adapted to every condition of life, and recommended as the

will and reason of the Supreme Deity, and enforced
by the sanction of eternal rewards and punishments."

" For this—of all that ever influenced man,
  Since Abel worshipped or the world began,
  This only spares no lust ; admits no plea ;
  But makes him, if at all, completely free,
  Sounds forth the signal, as she mounts her car,
  Of an eternal, universal war :
  Rejects all treaty ; penetrates all wiles ;
  Scorns with the same indifference frowns and smiles ;
  Drives through the realms of sin, where riot reels,
  And grinds his crown beneath her burning wheels."

VI. THE PERSON OF CHRIST IS THE ATTRACTION
OF THE GOSPEL.—It is related of a certain artist in
Germany that he desired to make a bust of Christ,
so that His character might be expressed in His
countenance.   When he had finished it, he was
anxious to know if he had given a correct expression
to the features.   He therefore called in a Sunday
school scholar, and pointing to the statue, asked him
who it was.   The boy said he did not know, but supposed that it must be some great king.   At once
the artist knew that he had failed to procure the
resemblance he desired ; he therefore set to work
again, and when he had finished his work the second
time he called the boy in, and put the same question
as before.   Immediately the boy replied, " That is my
blessed Saviour."

As the artist was able so to form the clay to
resemble the features of Christ that the boy recognized Him, so the Gospel presents to us—not a
resemblance of Christ, but the loving Person of
Christ, and this is the loadstone of the Gospel.   It

speaks of, reveals, and brings to us the living Christ, whose touch is life-giving and healing; whose words are soothing and strengthening; whose love is permanent and prevailing; and whose Person is as attractive to the spiritual mind as the law of gravitation to the earth.

VII. LOVE IS THE ATMOSPHERE OF THE GOSPEL. —As the atmosphere is the means of the radiation of the sun, making its warming rays to fall gently upon us, so the Gospel brings to us the glad tidings of God's love, which pours into our being, as the sun's rays into the greenhouse, warming and fertilizing. As the atmosphere contains all the constituents that go to make up the body, so the love of God is the element in which we should live that our spiritual being may be healthful and happy. If we would have the love of holiness, we must abide in the holiness of love; and if we would have the love of truth, we must keep in the truth of love; and if we would have the love of communion, we must walk in the communion of love.

VIII. THE COMING OF CHRIST IS THE APEX OF THE GOSPEL.—On the tomb of Dr. John Conder, in Bunhill Fields, in the City of London, is this inscription:—

"I HAVE SINNED,

"I HAVE TRUSTED,

"I HAVE REPENTED,

"I HAVE LOVED,

"I REST,

"I SHALL RISE.

" AND THROUGH THE GRACE OF

"CHRIST, HOWEVER UNWORTHY,   I SHALL REIGN."

In the last sentence, " I shall reign," we have the hope of the Christian which is founded on the promise of Christ. It was remarked to the writer recently that it was a very unusual thing for the coming of Christ to be preached upon, and that in not doing so the Gospel was not fully preached. The writer fully concurred. The Gospel of God is called " the Gospel of the glory of Christ " (2 Cor. iv. 4, R.V.), and as the " Gospel of the glory of Christ " it specially refers to His coming again.

Thanks be to God for His Gospel ! As the Son of God in His death and resurrection is the axis of the Gospel, so let all our life centre in Him. As the faith of God is the means by which we are saved, so let us trust in Him alone. As the Spirit of God is the Applier of the Gospel, so let us seek Him to apply all the truths of the Gospel to us. As the holiness of God is that which is enjoined upon us to be reproduced in our conduct, so let us open our hearts to Christ that He in His holiness may dwell therein. As the Beloved of God is the attraction of the Gospel, so let us prize Him above all. As the love of God is the atmosphere of the Gospel, so let us abide in His love. And as the promise of God in the return of His Son is the apex of the Gospel, so let us look for Him, patiently, watchfully, and prayerfully.

EIGHT NEGATIVES

" Not been found vain."

" Not of error."

" Nor of uncleanness."

" Nor in guile."

" Not as pleasing men."

" Neither at any time were we found using words of flattery."

" Nor a cloke of covetousness."

" Nor seeking glory of men " (1 Thess. 2:1,3,4,5,6 R.V.)

12

EIGHT NEGATIVES

AMONG the many things that impress the reader of the Epistles of the Apostle Paul is their genuine ring. There is no man who uses the capital "I" more than he does, and yet he does it in such a manner as not to attract attention to himself, but to the Lord. He is like the atmosphere, which, while it transmits the rays of the sun, is unseen itself.

There was no need for the Apostle to defend his apostleship with the Church at Thessalonica, as there was at Corinth; but still, on the other hand, he does not forget to remind the saints how he and his fellow-labourers behaved themselves among them. We shall call attention to the negative side of their work first, or how they did not preach and practise. There are eight negatives.

I. NOT UNREALLY. —"Our entering in unto you hath not been found vain." The Authorized Version gives the thought that the Gospel was successful in the fruits that were seen in those who received it; whereas the Revised undoubtedly draws attention to the manner in which the servants of Christ came to them. It is the latter sense which is to be taken.

It is to " the character of the entrance, not to the fruits, to its fulness of power and purpose and reality," that reference is made. Stephen, when before the council delivering his burning message, was very real. There were no empty words. He was not as an empty bladder, but as a solid rock. Now, although he was all this, yet he was not apparently successful, for his message was not received. To give utterance to things that are true is no proof that we are true ; and to be true, and yet not be successful, is no slur on our reality. To be is more important than to say; for to be is to say in the most powerful way, as the house that is founded on the rock by its weathering the storm tells out its stability.

II. NOT ERRONEOUSLY.—" Not of error." He was not deceived, neither was he deceiving. His teaching was not only right, but the way in which he did it was right also. " He was so assured of the truth of the Gospel, and of the integrity of his own motives, that he proclaimed it everywhere and at all hazards." We read of those who receive not the love of the truth that they might be saved, that God shall send them a " strong delusion " (" error," R.V.) that they shall believe a lie (2 Thess. ii. 11). As God shall send to the hearts of these unbelieving ones " the working of error," so God had sent into Paul's heart the conviction of the truth of the Gospel, so that his exhortation, instead of being like Balaam's error, leading to destruction, was as the beacon light which directs the mariner to avoid the dangerous coast, and to steer into the harbour of refuge.

III. NOT UNHOLILY.—" Nor of uncleanness,"

Christ had to say to the Pharisees that, while they were fair and beautiful on the exterior, internally they were full of filthiness. He compares them to whited sepulchres, which are beautiful outside, but inside full of dead men's bones and all uncleanness. These servants of God were the contrast to this. They were pure in heart as to their inner life, they were pure in motive as to their Christian service, and they exemplified what they taught. They not only *said* "Be clean," but they *were* clean. The uncleanness of covetousness, the uncleanness of selfishness, the uncleanness of worldliness, the uncleanness of worldly applause, and all the kindred tribe, must not be in the heart and lives of those whom God has called to be His witnesses.

IV. NOT DECEITFULLY.—"Nor in guile." The Apostles did not act in any way on the principle that the end justifies the means. All their actions were in simplicity and godly sincerity. What an amount of guile there is practised to-day in connection with so-called Christian work! "Call birds" is an expression that is used in some evangelistic meetings, when one professes to be anxious, that he may induce others to follow his example. Such work will not stand the test of the judgment seat of Christ. When the materials of deceit are used, the building will not be well and substantially built. As Archbishop Whately says, "It is difficult to maintain falsehood. When the materials of a building are solid blocks of stone, very rude architecture will suffice; but a structure of rotten materials needs the most careful adjustment in order to make it stand."

V. Not for the approval of man.—"Not as pleasing men." The desire was not to win human applause. They could not descend to such a low level. They were actuated by higher principles and purer motives. *If we do not seek to please men, we must not be surprised if we displease them.* It is related of a certain preacher that he greatly offended the king by his direct utterances when preaching before him on one occasion. The king sent for him and said,—

"Massillon, you have greatly offended me."

"That is what I wished to do, sire," replied the preacher.

The principle is true in practice as well as in preaching, for if we faithfully tell out the truth of the Gospel and truthfully manifest it in our lives, we shall be sure to be an offence to some, and ungodly men will say to us, as Ahab to Elijah, "Art thou he that troubleth Israel?" *Again, if we do not seek to please men, we shall glorify God.* One has well said, in speaking of Paul's devotion, "Brave Paul! he spoke the Word, whether sinners would hear or not, whether men were converted or not. If it pleased God he was content." Just like that grand man who kept working away in isolation in the heart of China, and for years saw no conversion. A lady said to him, "What good are you doing in China, Mr. Burns?" To which he replied, "Madam, I did not go to China to convert the Chinese, I went to glorify God." He went to serve and please his Master.

I was asked to examine a young man who wanted to give up his business and go to Africa as a missionary. I asked him, " What is your motive in wanting to take this step ? Suppose you were to go to the heart of Africa, and see thousands bowing down before their idols, and refusing to hear of Christ, what would you do ?"

He replied, " I'd just keep pegging away."

That is the right spirit of service : to keep pegging away for the Master, not to please the society, not to have a large place on the statistics, not to have a great following, but to please God. If we go forth to any service according to the will of God, and only to please Him, He will bless us in our souls, and in the end give us to see His power in the salvation of sinners.

VI. NOT FLATTERINGLY.—" Neither at any time were we found using words of flattery." These servants of God did not pick and choose their words. Flattery is to say what is not true of another. It is to trade with false money, which would not be current were it not for the pride of man. He who plays the part of flatterer is neither a benefit to the flattered nor a blessing to himself. The fable of the chameleon and porcupine illustrates this : A chameleon once met a porcupine, and complained that he had taken great pains to make friends with everybody ; but, strange to say, he had entirely failed, and could not now be sure that he had a friend in the world. " And by what means," said the porcupine, " have you sought to make friends ?" " By flattery," said the chameleon. " I have adapted myself to all I have met ; humoured the follies and foibles of every one. In order to make people believe I liked them, I have imitated their manners, as if I considered them models of perfection. So far have I gone in this that it has become a habit for me; and now my very skin takes the hue and complexion of the thing that happens to be nearest. Yet all this has been in vain; for everybody calls me a turncoat, and I am generally considered selfish, hypocritical, and base." "And no doubt you deserve all this," said the porcupine. I have taken a different course, but I must confess that I have as few friends as you. I have adopted the rule to resent every encroachment upon my dignity. I would allow no one even to touch me without sticking into him one of my sharp quills. I determined to take care of number one, and the result has been that, while I have vindicated my rights, I have created a universal dislike. I am called ' Old Touch-me-not,' and if I am not as much despised I am even more disliked than you, Sir Chameleon."

VII. NOT COVETOUSLY.—" Nor a cloke of covetousness." Paul and his fellow-labourers seem to say, " We did not do one thing to cover up another. We did not mask our real feelings." For one to use a cloak of covetousness is to be like the sailors of whom we read in Acts xxvii. 30, who, under pretence of casting the anchors out of the ship, meant to escape from it. A preacher who seeks to please that he may obtain money wears a cloak of covetousness. A man who asks for admission to a Christian church, that he may have a better opportunity of making known his business or theories, wears a cloak of covetousness. A man believing one thing while in fellowship with a church believing the opposite wears a cloak of covetousness. A tradesman who represents an article to be one thing when it is different wears a cloak of covetousness.

VIII. NOT SEEKING FOR HUMAN APPLAUSE.—" Nor seeking glory of men, neither from you, nor from others, when we might have claimed honour " (margin, R.V.) "as apostles of Christ." Chrysostom explains these words as follows :—" Not seeking honour nor boasting ourselves, nor requiring attention of guards. And yet, even if we had done this, we had done nothing out of character, for if persons sent by mere earthly kings are in honour, much more might we be." All spiritually-minded men and women have always seen the emptiness of mere human applause. Fénelon well said, "I love a serious preacher, who speaks for my sake, and not his own glory."

It is related of a certain pilot in a storm, that he looked up to heaven, as his boat was being tossed about by the stormy waves, and said, "Neptune, you may sink or save me, but I will hold my rudder true." Let us each in the strength of God say, "I will hold the rudder of my life true to the Lord who has been so true to me."

" But having suffered before, and been shamefully entreated, as ye know, at Philippi, we waxed bold in our God to speak unto you the Gospel of God in much conflict. . . . We were gentle in the midst of you, as when a nurse cherisheth her own children : even so, being affectionately desirous of you, we were well pleased to impart unto you, not the Gospel of God only, but also our own souls, because ye were become very dear to us. For ye remember, brethren, our labour and travail : working night and day, that we might not burden any of you, we preached unto you the Gospel of God. Ye are witnesses, and God also, how holily and righteously and unblameably we behaved ourselves toward you that believe " (1 Thess. 2:2,7-10 R.V.)

13
HOW THE APOSTLES BEHAVED

WHAT a man is impresses all he does. Character is the type that prints itself on the page of the man's actions. If an author is a good man, it will be seen in the words he writes. If a tradesman is righteous, the sixteen ounces to the pound will evidence it. If a man is a believer in Christ, Christ-likeness shows that he is in Christ. That what a man is impresses all he does is clearly brought out in the lives of the three devoted servants of Christ who planted the Church at Thessalonica, for Paul not only said what they were, but they were what he said.

How did they behave themselves?

I. BOLDLY OR CONFIDENTLY.—"We waxed bold." There was no hesitation or equivocation on the part of the servants of Christ, for they believed what they said—hence there was the accent of conviction. Their utterances were as a rough file that made the consciences of men to smart; their words were as a knife to cut out the gangrene of sin; and their preaching was as a trumpet blast that aroused men to repentance or inflamed with rage, as is always the

case when the truth is declared in the boldness of
the Holy Spirit and the confidence in God which is
its cause.   That this is so may be clearly apprehended if we call to mind the fact that the three
thousand who were "pricked to the heart" on the
day of Pentecost, were converted, and the members
of the council who were "cut to the heart" by the
burning words of Stephen were filled with hatred
against him (Acts ii. 37 ; vii. 54).

II. IN COMMUNION WITH GOD.—"We waxed bold
in our God."   In Chapter I. 1, we have "the Church
in God," that is the believer's position as one who is
saved by grace ; but here we have the believer's
element as the servant of God.   There is a boldness
which may be for God, but not "in God," as in the
case of Peter when he cut off the ear of the servant
of the high priest.   Boldness in God means at least
four things.   First, *confidence before God*, which
grows in the soil of an uncondemning heart (1 John
iii. 21, R.V.).   Second, *Courage for God*, which
comes from the inspiration that is begotten by the
love of God.   His love for us causes us to show our
love for Him, as David's mighty men, who out of love
for him cut their way through the host of the Philistines to get a drink of water from the well at
Beth-lehem.   Third, *Consecration to God*, which is
as a spring that causes the machinery of our nature
to keep time with the sun of God's truth.   Fourth,
Communion with God, as the husband and wife
living in the one house have all things in common,
and mutually consult the welfare of each other.

III. ENDURINGLY.—"In much conflict."   Acts xvi.

tells as how shamefully ill-treated these servants of God were at Philippi. They were scourged, cast into the inner prison, and their feet made fast in the stocks. At Thessalonica they met with much opposition while they were preaching; the unbelieving Jews would have done them injury; they were charged with turning the world upside down and acting contrary to the decrees of Cæsar (Acts xvii. 1-9) But in spite of all this they steadily kept on their way, like an Atlantic liner in the face of a storm. A German professor has lately made experiments with chalcedony and other quartzose minerals, and he has demonstrated that when such stones are ground on large and rapidly revolving wheels, they exhibit a brilliant phosphorescent glow throughout their entire mass. So is it with the resolute worker. The more he is ground under the strong wheel of suffering and persecution, the more intensely will his character glow.

IV. GENTLY.—" But we were gentle in the midst of you, as when a nurse cherisheth her own children." There was no officialism about these servants of God. They were as a mother to these believers. The illustration is of a mother nursing her child, watching over it with tender regard, anticipating its wants, bearing with its wilfulness, studying its welfare, hushing its cry, and looking after its interest. In this we have a pattern for older Christians to imitate in their dealings with their younger brethren.

It becomes believers in all their relations with each other to be gentle. And what a power there is in gentleness! As one has said, " There is a power in gentleness to subdue the mightiest opposition, and to triumph over the most gigantic difficulties. The gentle rays of the sun melt the ponderous iceberg more speedily than the rolling billows of an angry ocean; the silent action of the atmosphere wastes the rock which remains immovable under the strokes of the heaviest weapon. A look from Moses vanquished the calf idolatry of the Israelites, which the fluent eloquence of Aaron had been powerless to resist; a calm, quiet word from Jesus paralyzed with fear the band of soldiers who came to arrest Him in Gethsemane. True gentleness is never weak. It is the tough, indestructible material out of which are formed the hero and the martyr." At the Synod of Moscow, held by King Goutram, A.D. 585, bishops were forbidden to keep dogs in their houses or birds of prey, lest the poor should be bit by these animals instead of being fed. Should not all Christians keep from angry tempers, repulsive manners, and morose habits, lest others should be hurt and hindered? Yea, they will if they are believers in truth.

V. AFFECTIONATELY.—"Even so, being affectionately desirous of you, we were well pleased to impart unto you, not the Gospel of God only, but also our own souls, because ye were become very dear to us." This was no mere sentimental expression, but a statement that had been demonstrated by the patience under provocation, the perseverance under difficulties, and the consuming zeal and holy passion of soul that had constrained these devoted men of God to act as they did. Yea, these servants of God seem to say, " As a nursing mother would not only impart her milk to her children, but risk her life for them, so we not only imparted gladly the spiritual milk of the Word to you, but risked our lives for your spiritual nourishment, imitating Him who laid down His life for us." And the reason of all their interest in and intensity for those at Thessalonica was because they were dear unto them. As Trapp says, " Honing and hankering after you : the Greek word signifieth the most swaying heart-passion, the most effectual affection." Love is the power that overcomes difficulties, yea, that makes impossibilities possibilities, possibilities probabilities, and probabilities certainties.

VI. TOILINGLY.—" For ye remember, brethren, our labour and travail : working night and day, that we might not burden any of you, we preached unto you the Gospel of God." The word " labour " means toil —hard work. The same term is used in the parable of the importunate widow, where the unjust judge is being troubled and wearied by the woman's importunity. The judge is made to say, in reluctantly granting the widow's request, " Though I fear not God, nor regard man; yet because this widow *troubleth* me, I will avenge her, lest she wear me out by her continual coming " (Luke xviii. 5, R.V.). What the Apostle meant to say was, " We gave ourselves up to daily and nightly drudgery, which wholly absorbed all our physical powers, for your sakes." He further illustrates the laboriousness of their life service by speaking of its " travail " as well as its toil. Ellicott says that " the first word marks the toil on the side of the suffering it involves, and the latter on the side of the magnitude of the obstacles it has to overcome." Thus the soldier in a campaign has much toil as he is on the march, but when he meets the enemy it is a struggle to the death, if need be. Undoubtedly the word " travail " is meant to intensify the term " labour." The one grows out of the other as the twig proceeds out of the branch. Hence we generally find the two words together, as in 2 Cor. xi. 27 and 2 Thess. iii. 8. Eadie says, " The phrase is a terse and familiar idiom. It will therefore denote toil even to weariness, labour to even utter exhaustion, comprising alike the work which he did as the Apostle, and the fatigue endured by the effort to support himself by manual industry." That this is meant is clearly brought out by the words, " Working night and day, that we might not be a burden to any of you." Why the Apostle gave up his claim to personal maintenance we cannot say. It could not have been because the Church at Thessalonica was poor, for there were " Greek women of honourable estate, and of men not a few" (Acts xvii. 12, R.V.). In all probability he was " anxious that he might not be misinterpreted, or the purity of his motives challenged, and that he might not be likened to a selfish and grasping sophist, to whom hire was everything, and therefore he would take nothing in compensation, but toiled to support himself, that the Gospel without hindrance, and in an unselfish and disinterested form, might win its way among the Gentiles." The spirit that animated these servants of Christ should fill us all. The love of Christ was the motive power that moved the hearts of these men. It was not for what they escaped by believing in Christ, not for what they enjoyed in the spiritual blessing conferred upon them, not for what they hoped to have in the future kingdom and glory of Christ, not for any spiritual power they might possess, not for any social position they might reach, not to draw attention to themselves as in the case of Simon Magus, but simply and solely out of love to the Saviour, who had given Himself for them, that they toiled as they did.

VII. CONSISTENTLY.—" Ye are witnesses, and God also, how holily and righteously and unblameably we behaved ourselves toward you that believe." Here we have a trinity of characteristics in relation to the manner of Paul and his co-workers towards those that believed.

They behaved themselves *holily,* for they remembered that they were responsible to God. Their manner was like pure gold, free from the alloy of self-interest and self-display. Their manner was as the sunlight which streams upon the traveller as he journeys along the country road, and not as the sunlight which comes through the cathedral window, coloured by the stained glass. The secret of this holy manner is to remember our relation to the Holy One. A holy man is a whole man, one whose whole being is concentrated upon God. As the priests of old were to act in a priestly manner as God's representatives towards others, and not to do anything in a way that was unbecoming to the office which they held, so the saints of God are ever to act in a saintly manner towards each other.

The Apostles acted *righteously.* There was no crookedness in their behaviour. There was no saying one thing and believing another; or believing anything, and keeping back part of the price, as Ananias. The one who acts righteously is jealous for the honour and glory of God, as Phinehas when he killed the iniquitous persons who were defiling the camp of Israel by their sin. The one who acts justly will do to others as he would that others would to him. As Nathan acted righteously when he told David of his sin, and as Jonathan dealt truly when he told David that he would fill the place that should have been his own, so the one who acts justly will not fail to tell others of their sin, and be ready to give up to others that which would have been of advantage to himself.

The Apostles behaved *unblameably*. There was no spot in the sun of their methods. The tone of their conduct was holy. The temper of their style was right. The fashion of their action was blameless. These men of God could appeal to God, and to the believers, that they acted as they stated. It could never be said of them as was said of Baron de Joest, of Paris, who died in 1887, leaving £100,000 to the Society for the Prevention of Cruelty to Animals, "He belonged to seventeen different humanitarian societies, but showed little benevolence to man or beast during his life-time."

DEALING AND DEPORTMENT

"As ye know how we dealt with each one of you, as a father with his own children, exhorting you, and encouraging you, and testifying, to the end that ye should walk worthily of God, who calleth you into His own kingdom and glory" (1 Thess. 2:11,12 R.V.)

14
DEALING AND DEPORTMENT

IT is said of a Roman prince of the house of
Colonna, whose unsullied character had sustained
him alike in times of prosperity and persecution,
when driven into exile, that he was asked,
"Where is now your fortress?" He laid his hand
upon his breast, and exclaimed, "Here!" A con-
scious sense of uprightness threw a halo of
strength and majesty around him in the midst
of his sufferings. In like manner an inward
knowledge of purity constrained the Apostles to
appeal to those among whom they had laboured,
that they were desirous of the welfare of the
Lord's people alone. This is self-evident, if we
remember that the end of the teaching of these
servants of God was that the saints might walk
worthily of God.

I. THE DEALING OF THE APOSTLES AS A FATHER
TOWARDS HIS CHILDREN. — "Ye then know how we
dealt with each one of you, as a father with
his own children," etc. There is a fourfold
manner of the dealing of the Apostles, as
illustrated in a father's action towards his
children. First, it was individual dealing.
"Each one of you." The late C. H. Spurgeon
used to be called, in connection with the

Pastors' Evangelical Conference, not merely "the President," but "the Pastor-President." This was because each member of the Conference felt that he took an individual interest in him. What Paul said to the elders at Ephesus,—that he taught them from "house to house" (Acts xx. 20), may be applied to the saints at Thessalonica. This individual interest should be manifested, not only by the pastor to the people, but by each saint to each other. Second, it was *earnest dealing*—"exhorted." They did not give dull directions, but direct and fervent appeals. Their exhortations were earnest and faithful, like the yearning importunity of a mother's heart, or the fresh, familiar, loving counsels breathed from a father's lips. Third, it was *encouraging dealing*—"encouraging." The meaning of the word "encouraging" is *coming alongside to help.* As Eliezer helped and guided Rebekah from her home till she met with Isaac, so believers should help each other. Christians should not be damps. It is said that we are not to "quench the Spirit;" that is, we are not to seek to extinguish or diminish the light in others. Fourth, it was *faithful dealing* — "testifying." They solemnly adjured the saints, as in the Lord's presence, to be true to Him. As John the Baptist was a bright and shining light, because he faithfully bare record of the truth, so every Christian should truly witness with life and lips that he knows and walks with Him who is the Truth.

II. THE DEPORTMENT OF BELIEVERS AS WALKING WORTHILY OF THE LORD WAS THE END THAT THE APOSTLES HAD IN VIEW IN DEALING WITH THE SAINTS

AS THEY DID.—"To the end that ye should walk worthily of God." There are five other places where the word "worthily" occurs in connection with the conduct of those who are related to the Lord, and we draw attention to these passages of Scripture as illustrating what it is to walk worthily of God.

1. *To walk worthily of God is to show kindness to those who are the Lord's.* "I commend unto you Phœbe our sister . . . that ye receive her in the Lord, *worthily* of the saints, and that ye assist her in whatsoever matter she may have need of you, for she herself also hath been a succourer of many, and of mine own self" (Rom. xvi. 1, 2, R.V.). Thus does the Apostle Paul commend the deaconess Phœbe to the saints at Rome, and the Apostle John breathes the same spirit in writing to the beloved Gaius to extend kindness to strangers in the following words, "Beloved, thou doest a faithful work in whatsoever thou doest toward them that are brethren and strangers withal; who bare witness to thy love before the Church: whom thou wilt do well to set forward on their journey *worthily* of God, because that for the sake of the name they went forth, taking nothing of the Gentiles. We therefore ought to welcome such, that they may be fellow-workers with the truth" (3 John 5-8, R.V.).

Putting the above Scriptures together we apprehend that we act worthily of God as we are true to the name of saints which we bear. As of old it was said to a Roman emperor, "Remember thou art Cæsar," so as we call to mind that we are God's separated ones, we shall be interested in all who occupy the like position, for this is the evidence of our oneness in the mystical body of Christ.

2. *To walk worthily of God is for our whole behaviour to be in harmony with the Gospel.* " Behave as citizens *worthily* (margin) of the Gospel of Christ " (Philip. i. 27, R.V.).   " It was said of M'Cheyne that people felt him when he entered a meeting or private home.   Although not a stern, sanctimonious man, but a cheerful one, yet people recognized him as a man of God, who carried the atmosphere of heaven with him, and lived out the Gospel of Christ.   The inward spirit shone out from him, in his language and conduct, just as a blazing lamp always reports itself." What was said about M'Cheyne reminds us of some words of his own, " How diligently the cavalry officer keeps his sabre clean and sharp !   Every stain he removes with the greatest care.   Remember you are God's sword, His instrument, I trust a chosen vessel to bear His name, in great measure, according to the purity and perfectness of the instrument, will be success.   It is not great talents that God blesses so much as likeness to Jesus."   Mark   the   words   that   are   said   about M'Cheyne, " *He lived out the Gospel of Christ.*" What are the two main pillars of the Gospel ?   The death and resurrection of Christ.   And what are the practical outcomes of these facts to the one who believes in Christ ?   That he is dead to sin and alive unto God.   Dead to sin with its penalty, bondage, pleasures, and authority ; and alive unto God in His liberty, grace, and power.   The one who lives the Gospel walks worthy of it and preaches it in the best

sense of the word, for to be is to speak, as Lamartine
once said to a Parisian populace, when he introduced
to them an honest man, " Citizens, listen, for sixty
years of pure life is about to address you." The mob
stood silent. And in like manner all will acknowledge the power of the Gospel, when they behold the
Gospel in its power living in us.

3. *To walk worthily of God is to have our
general deportment towards our fellow-believers in
keeping with the key-note of the love of Christ.* " I
therefore, the prisoner in the Lord, beseech you to
walk worthily of the calling wherewith ye were called,
. . . with longsuffering, forbearing one another in
love" (Ephes. iv. 1, 2, R.V.). It is a remarkable and
God-honouring testimony that the son and biographer
of Cæsar Malan gives of his father as he speaks of his
home life :—" I never saw anything in him which
did not renew the impression that he lived to Him
who is invisible. Never was I witness to a gesture,
never did I hear a word with respect to which I had
to feel that it would become to him the subject of
serious regret." We would that the same could be
said of every believer. Oh that the lowliness of
humility, the meekness of patience, the longsuffering
of grace, and the forbearance of love, might be the
four horns of the altar to which the living sacrifice of
our life might be bound !

4. *To walk worthily of the Lord is to bear fruit
in all our work by seeking to please Him.* " To
walk worthily of the Lord unto all pleasing, bearing
fruit in every good work " (Col. i. 10, R.V.). Knowing God's will, it is for us to do it ; for if we know

His mind, and do not seek to carry out His desire, the knowledge will be a curse to us instead of a blessing, even as the uneaten manna that was left by the Israelites bred worms and stank. Eadie has well said, in speaking of the walk that is worthy of God:—" To walk worthy of the Lord is to feel the solemn bond of the redeeming blood; to enshrine the image of Him who shed it; to breathe His Spirit and act in harmony with His example; to exhibit His temperament in its elements of purity, piety, and love; to be in the world as He was in the world; to be good and to do good; and to show by the whole demeanour that His law is the rule that governs, and His glory the aim which elevates and directs." Have we walked worthily of our Father as His children, by implicitly trusting His word, as Caleb and Joshua, when, in spite of the fears of their brethren and the foes of Canaan, they said, " We are able to take the land ? " As God's children have we walked worthily of Him by obeying His every command, especially to be separated to Him alone, and to walk with Him as Enoch did, that He might initiate us in His ways even as He did His servant Moses, for " He made known His ways " unto him ? As the adopted sons of God do we walk worthily of Him by wearing the stamp of His holy character as the wax bears the impress of the die that has been pressed upon it ? As those who have been purchased by the blood of Christ do we walk worthily of Him, by remembering that we are not our own, that we have been bought with a price, and act accordingly ? As those who are united to the living Christ do we

walk worthily of Him, by allowing Him as our Life
to permeate our whole being, as the sap of the vine
fills the branch and manifests its fruitfulness through
it ? As those who are members of the mystical body
of Christ do we walk worthily of Him, who is the
Head, by allowing Him to prompt us to act toward
our fellow-members even as He would do toward us
Himself, that is, in love, in grace, in tenderness, in
sympathy, in tears, in prayers, and in help ? As
those who are the temples of the Holy Spirit do we
walk worthily of Him by allowing Him to enter every
chamber of our being as Lord and Governor of all ?
Oh that we may walk as we talk ! The reason why
there was such power in the early Church was
because the Christians were what they preached, as
one has said :—" There was one great secret of the
Apostles' power in winning converts to Christ ; *the
sermons wore shoes.* I honestly believe that one of
the chief reasons for the fewness of conversions to
Christ is that there is so little preaching for Christ
in the daily lives of His professed disciples, and such
a fearful amount of direct preaching against Him.
Actions speak louder than words. The bad sermons
of the life are an overmatch for the best sermons on
Sunday from the lips. Every life is a sermon. Paul
himself would not have had any converts to the
Gospel of the cross if he had not proved to the world
that ' Christ liveth in me.' His own heroic and holy
life was one of the grandest epistles he ever produced."

One great reason for the sad lack of conversions to
Christ in our day is, that so many of the sermons in

shoes lead the wrong way.   A true and noble life is the mightiest of discourses.   It is the sermons in shoes that must convert the world to Christ, if it is ever to be converted.   It is related of the good Saint Francis of Assisi that he once stepped down into the cloisters of his monastery, and, laying his hand on the shoulder of a young monk, said, " Brother, let us go down into the town and preach."   So they went forth, the venerable father and the young man.   And they walked along upon their way, conversing as they went.   They wound their way down the principal streets, round the lowly alleys and lanes, and even to the outskirts of the town, and to the villages beyond, till they found themselves back at the monastery again.   Then said the young monk, " Father, when shall we begin to preach ? "   And the father looked kindly down upon his son, and said, " My child, we have been preaching; we were preaching while we were walking.   We have been seen, looked at; our behaviour has been remarked; and so we have delivered a morning sermon.   Ah, my son, it is of no use that we walk anywhere to preach unless we preach as we walk."

5. *To walk worthily of the Lord is to behave our-selves as those who are called to His kingdom and glory.*   "Ye should walk worthily of God, who calleth you into His own kingdom and glory " (1 Thess. ii. 12, R.V.).   God, in wondrous love, did not spare His own Son when He gave Him as the sin-offering to die for us (Rom. viii. 32).   He has purchased us to Himself with His own blood (Acts xx. 28); and He calleth to His own kingdom and glory.   Mark the two things to

which believers are called—"kingdom" and "glory"—
the kingdom having reference to the realm into which
we shall be introduced when Christ comes, and the glory
indicating the position we shall occupy as reigning in
glorified bodies and exaltation with Him. Since we
are called to such honours, how should we honour
Him who has called us with such a high calling! As
princes of royal blood should be princely, so saints
who are called with such a heavenly calling should
live heavenly lives. It was said of Alexander the
Great that when he was asked to run in the Olympic
games, he exclaimed, "Do *kings* use to run at the
Olympics?" He felt it beneath his dignity to run in
the races. In like manner no Christian should do
anything that would compromise his position and
dignity as one who is of a higher realm than the
earth. "To walk worthily of God, who is calling us
to His kingdom and glory, is to have one's whole
course of life preserved in harmony with God's
gracious work upon the soul, and with the high and
hallowed destiny with which that work is lovingly
connected, and into which it is ever ripening."

"And for this cause we also thank God without ceasing, that, when ye received from us the Word of the message, *even the Word* of God, ye accepted *it* not *as* the word of men, but, as it is in truth, the Word of God, which also worketh in you that believe" (1 Thess. 2:13 R.V.)

15

A WONDERFUL CASKET
AND
A WISE COURSE

THERE have been many explanations as to what the Apostle refers to when he says, "For this cause," but we are inclined to believe with Alford that the words are related to the fact that God had called the believers to whom the Apostle was writing to the Lord's kingdom and glory. As Alford says, "Seeing that He is thus calling you, your thorough reception of the Word is to us a cause of thanksgiving to Him."

I. A WONDERFUL CASKET, "the Word of God," etc. There are many reasons that might be given as adducing the wonderfulness of the Word of God, but we limit ourselves to three.

1. The Word of God is wonderful because it is peculiar in its make. "When ye received from us the Word of the message, even the Word of God, ye accepted it not as the word of men, but, as it is in truth, the Word of God." If we leave out the underlined words we get a more positive statement: "When ye received from us the Word of the message of God, ye accepted not the word of men, but, as it is in truth, the Word of God." The word of men is as

fickle as the wind, changing with the current of popular thought, but the Word of God is as firm as a mountain of granite, and as immutable and as immovable as the eternal Rock of Ages. The Word of God is *living* in its *essence*. As the life-germ is in the propagating seed, so the Word of God is the seed by which the Divine life is implanted in the believer. The Word of God is *lasting* in its *nature*. As gold is always gold, and cannot be anything else, so the Word of truth is as unalterable as God Himself. The Word of God is *lovely* in its *structure*. Like a majestic temple beside a number of huts, resplendent in its beauty as the sun gilds its many spires and pinnacles, so this Book stands out above all other books. The Word of God is *lighting* in its *mission*. As the electric current flashes along the wire, and causes the carbon to ignite, so the Divine light by the Spirit of life through the Word inflames man's nature with a new desire, namely, love to God and man. The Word of God is *loving* in its *tone*. In it are heard the tender invitations of the compassionate Saviour, and the gracious calls of the holy God, which come like the affectionate pleadings of a mother to her child. The Word of God is *liberating* in its *action*. As the knife cuts the prisoner's bonds, and the kindly hand lifts the load from the burdened back, so the truth tells of the blood of Christ which removes the burden of sin from the conscience, and speaks of the power of Christ which gives deliverance from sin's dominion. The Word of God is *luring* in its *attraction*. It is not a wrecker's light luring to destruction, but a wondrous picture in which are seen the beauties of the skill of the heavenly Artist, and which charm and fascinate the beholder. The make of the Book must be wonderful, for the Maker Himself is wonderful. He who wrote it is perfect. His utterances are reliable and unerring. How unlike the words of men, which are uncertain and erring. Aristotle said, " There is no difference between what men call knowledge and mere opinion : therefore, as opinion is uncertain, there can be no certainty in human knowledge." Another has said, " Nothing can be known, nothing, therefore, can be learned ; nothing can be certain ; the senses are limited and delusive ; intellect is weak ; life is short." Contrast these sayings of the great thinkers among men with the greater than the greatest of all earth-born utterances, viz., the words of Christ, the Living Word, of whom His enemies had to confess that He spake with authority and power. If we listen to men we shall be disappointed, but if we hearken to God we shall be humbled and blessed. It is related of a lady who once listened to Ebenezer Erskine, not knowing who he was, that she was much impressed by his discourse. Having been informed of the preacher's name, she went the next Sunday to his own place of worship to hear him. But she felt none of those strong impressions she experienced on the former occasion. Wondering at this, she called on Mr. E., and, stating the case, asked what might be the reason of such a difference in her feelings. He replied, " Madam, the reason is this, last Sunday you went to hear Jesus Christ, but to-day you have come to hear Ebenezer Erskine."

2. *The Word of God is wonderful because of the priceless jewels it contains.* It is related of a certain prince, who was in love with a handsome princess, that he sent her a beautiful casket of surpassing workmanship. When the princess opened it, all that it seemed to contain was a silver egg. In disgust the princess flung it to the ground, and as it fell a hidden spring was touched, and the silver egg opened and revealed a yolk of gold. The curiosity of the princess being aroused she began to press the yolk of gold, thinking that there might be further secrets in the present from the prince. Presently another spring was touched, and this time a miniature crown was revealed studded with priceless gems. Again another spring was touched, and inside the crown there was a splendid diamond engagement ring, which was a dumb appeal from the prince that the princess should marry him. In like manner, when we open the wondrous and God-wrought casket of God's Word, as the Holy Spirit enables us to touch the hidden springs, we see untold wealth and priceless jewels. The first jewel that we discover is the silver of redemption, telling us that there is liberty from the sentence and slavery of sin, through faith in the great Redeemer—Christ. Next we apprehend that there is the gold of relationship, for, in receiving Christ we are made the children of God. Then there is the crown of royalty, for, being Christ's, we are made kings and priests unto God ; and there is the ring of God's eternal love, by which we are wedded to Himself, from whom no earthly or hellish power can ever separate us. May we pray with the Psalmist,

" Open Thou mine eyes, that I may behold wondrous things out of Thy law " (Psalm cxix. 18), for there are wondrous things to be seen there, if we have the anointing of the Holy Spirit to enable us to see them, as there must be a spiritual mind led by the spiritual Teacher—the Holy Spirit—to understand this spiritual Book.

3. *The Word of God is wonderful because of the power it exerts.* " Which effectually worketh in you that believe."   Whatever the Word demands it provides, as one has said, " As the planet receiving the light of the sun is transformed into an imitation sun, so the believing soul, receiving the light of the Word, is changed into the image of that Word. Whatever the Divine Word prescribes, that it works in us.   Does it prescribe repentance ? it works repentance ; faith ? it works faith ; obedience ? it works obedience ; knowledge ? it lightens to know. Its transforming power is continually demonstrated. It makes the niggardly generous, the profane holy, the drunkard sober, the profligate chaste."   But, more than this, the Word imparts its own nature to those who are under its sovereign sway.   As the leaven which is put into the flour permeates the dough till the whole lump is leavened, so the Holy Word of God touches the whole nature of man : thus his mind is occupied with holy things, his feet are found walking in a holy way, his hands are uplifted in prayer in a holy manner, his eyes are directed to the Holy One, and he is indwelt by the Holy Spirit.

II. A WISE COURSE.—When the Apostle came with the Word of the Gospel, those whom he is addressing did three things, namely, they heard, received, and believed. There are three things that are suggested by their action, and these are, an opened ear, a receptive mind, and a responsive heart.

1. *An opened ear.* " Ye heard." There are hearers and hearers, as the parable of the sower plainly shows. The true and false hearer are strikingly referred to by Swinnock in the following words: —" Some hear the minister as chickens hear the hen; the hen calls them to come to her: they lie scraping in the dust, and will not hear her, till the kite cometh and devoureth them. But when the Word cometh with power, the soul heareth it, as Peter heard the cock; he goeth out and weepeth bitterly when he hears of the boundless mercy he hath deserted, the matchless misery he hath deserved, and the infinite love he hath abused. When we are hearing, like the Thessalonians, our souls must be changed into the similitude of the Word that it may come to us with power." Of the former class it must be said, " Having ears they hear not," but it may be said of the latter what Christ is made to say in prophecy, " Mine ears hast Thou opened :   .   .   .   I delight to do Thy will, O my God : yea, Thy law is within my heart " (Psalm xl. 6, 8). An opened ear is an honest and good heart which is willing to receive the good seed of the Word.

2. *A receptive mind.* " Ye accepted the Word of God." This is connected with, and is the result of, the ear opened by the Holy Spirit. Senaclæus said of the speech of Diarius the martyr, " Methought when I heard him speak, I heard the Holy Ghost

Himself preaching to me." The one who has the opened ear and receptive mind does hear the Holy Ghost speak when the Word of God is proclaimed. The receptive mind is the good soil which has room for the germinating seed of the truth which brings with it the life of God, so that the good ground is the soil where the fruit of the Spirit is rooted, and which fills the life with grace and love. The receptive mind is like the prepared slab under which the fragrant flowers are put that the preparation may absorb their sweetness, which after another process comes to us in the sweet-smelling perfume of the fragrant scents. We can only obtain the perfume of the Word as that Word dwells in us richly, and as it thus dwells in us the fragrance of the truth betrays itself, and others take knowledge of us that we have been with Jesus and have learned of Him. The receptive mind is like a good appetite, which relishes a good and wholesome meal, and needs not the got-up dishes of "modern thought," but is content with the pure and unadulterated Word of the truth of the Gospel.

3. *A responsive heart.* "The Word of God, which worketh in you that believe." As the well-made and well-kept machinery responds to the steam engine, so the believer who receives the truth in the love of it yields to and works with Him who is the Spirit of Truth. As the healthy member in the body obeys the willing of the head, so those who are members of Christ are under His direction and heartily respond to His Word. As the child shows its love to the father by the prompt obedience that is characteristic of it, so in like manner we declare our regard and

love to our Father when we obey Him fully as Caleb did.   Let us ever cheerfully respond to the Word of Christ by loving His sayings, treasuring up His words, and at once without any hesitation or compromise carrying out His commands.

PERSECUTION

" For ye, brethren, became imitators of the Churches of God
which are in Judæa in Christ Jesus : for ye also suffered the
same things of your own countrymen, even as they did of the
Jews" (1 Thess. 2:14)

16
PERSECUTION

THERE are two seeds mentioned in the Word of God which are as distinct as light and darkness, and these are the children of God and the children of the wicked one. By type, by statement, and by fact, they are brought before us, and are as patent as two rivers running side by side, the one being beautiful and clear, and the other muddy and loathsome. The one characteristic of the seed of the evil one, like a deadly serpent waiting for its prey, is to persecute the godly seed. Cain hates Abel, and slays him; the seed of the serpent entraps the sons of Seth, who call upon the name of the Lord, and corrupts them; Ishmael is jealous of Issac, and mocks him; the Egyptians rule the seed of Jacob, and oppress them; Amalek crosses the path of Israel, and seeks to overthrow him; Goliath defies the army of God, and sneers at the God of Israel; Saul plots against David, and schemes to kill him; Haman hates Mordecai, and would exterminate the seed of Israel to be rid of him; the children of the devil oppose the children of God, and as they killed the prophets, murdered the Lord Jesus, persecuted the Apostles, and caused the early

Christians to suffer, so the same spirit lies smouldering in the hearts of the children of the wicked one to-day, although they may have the mask of a smiling face over the hateful expression that is stamped on their true countenance. But as Samson said of the honey and the dead lion, " Out of the eater came forth meat, and out of the strong came forth sweetness;" so all the opposition with which the children of God are met the Lord overrules for their blessing. There are three ways in which we shall look at persecution :—As a *test*, as a *testimony*, as a *triumph.*

I. Persecution as a test.—A good workman will always test his work to see that it is able to meet the end for which it is designed and made. In like manner the Lord overrules the persecution of wicked men for the blessing of His people ; for the ungodly, by their persecution, but make the reality of the believer's allegiance to Christ the more manifest, even as the rubbing of the brass plate but makes it shine the brighter.

1. *Persecution tests the reality of our faith.* It is characteristic of the stony ground hearer that in the time of persecution he is offended, and, like the washed sow, goes back to his wallowing in the mire. Now with the true child of God persecution but acts as the cauldron of boiling lead to the traditional mouse of Agrippa, which would never wake till cast therein. Persecution rouses the latent faith in the believer, and he shows that he is of the royal mint of heaven, in that he rejoices that he is counted worthy to suffer for the name of Christ.

2. *Persecution tests the stability of our love.*
How many have been willing to part with life rather
than deny the Saviour! The noble army of martyrs
would rather die than deny their Lord. For Christ
and the Covenant, the Covenanters were hunted like
partridges, and would sooner have their brains blown
out—as cruel Claverhouse did John Brown's—than
give up the truth of God; or be tied to the stake as
those noble women in Wigtown Bay, and be tortured
as they were while they watched the incoming tide,
which slowly crept up as a mocking monster, and
surrounded them as a wet shroud to suffocate them;
thus gladly did they give up their lives out of love to
Christ. Persecution is like the storm to the oak to
the one who loves Christ, it but makes the roots of
our affection take a firmer hold in the soil of His
love. Christ is first with those who truly love Him;
as John Huss said, in lamenting the rupture of an
old and valued friendship, " Paletz is my friend, and
truth is my friend; and both being my friends, it is
my sacred duty to give honour to truth."

3. *Persecution tests the durability of our character.* Persecution, instead of blackening the characters of the three Hebrew young men, but made
them shine out the purer and brighter. It is said
that " on the destruction of the London Alexandra
Palace by fire it was found that, while many speci-
mens of old English porcelain exhibited there were
reduced to a black, shapeless mass, the true porcelain
of Bristol, though broken into fragments, still re-
tained its whiteness, and even its most delicate
shades of colour, uninjured by the fire. So the truly

good, though wounded, shall survive the fiercest trial, and retain intact all that distinguishes the Christian character."

II. PERSECUTION AS AN OPPORTUNITY FOR TESTIMONY.—There is the testimony which we are privileged to bear as we tell to others what the Lord has done for us, as the demoniac, who went home and told what great things the Lord had done for him; and there is the more powerful testimony we bear when we quietly, and patiently, and in a Christlike manner, endure the jest, the contemptuous sneer, the cruel words, the slanderous expression, the biting sarcasm, the goading ridicule, and the lying accusation; and as we thus patiently endure reviling we bear a twofold testimony. It is a testimony that we are the Lord's, and it is a testimony for the Lord.

1. *Persecution borne in the spirit of Christ is a testimony that we are the Lord's.* Spencer truly says, "A wolf flies not upon a painted sheep, and men can look upon a painted toad with delight. It is not the soft pace, but the furious march of the soldier that sets men a-gazing and dogs a-barking. Let but a man glide along with the stream of the world, do as others do, he may sit down and take his ease; but if he once strive against the stream, stand up in the cause of God, and act for Christ, then he shall be sure to meet with as much malice as men and devils can possibly throw upon him." The Israelites are opposed by the Amalekites and harassed by the Canaanites as soon as they come out of Egypt; and no sooner does one declare himself on the Lord's side than the evil one sets Mr. Worldly-Wiseman to lead him astray;

Mr. Flatterer to entrap him, Mr. Mistrust to scare him, Mr. Atheist to laugh at him, and Mr. Giant-Despair to imprison him, but all this plainly declares that we are on the side of Christ, for if we were not Satan would not trouble us.

2. *Persecution borne in the spirit of Christ is a testimony for the Lord.* As the barking of the dog makes the child run to its mother, so the persecution of the world but drives us to Christ. Cawdray well says in speaking of the benefit of persecution :—" As frankincense, when it is put into the fire, giveth the greater perfume ; as spice, if it be pounded and beaten, smelleth the sweeter; as the earth, when it is torn up by the plough, becometh the more fruitful ; the seed in the ground, after frost and snow and winter storms, springeth the ranker; the nigher the vine is pruned to the stock, the greater grape it yieldeth ; the grape, when it is most pressed and beaten maketh the sweeter wine; linen, when it is bucked and washed, wrung and beaten, is so made fairer and whiter ; even so the children of God receive great benefit by persecution; for by it God washeth and scoureth, schooleth and nourisheth them, that so, through many tribulations, they may enter into their rest." And as men watch the Christian in the time of persecution as he gladly and patiently suffers for Christ, they are impressed with the fact that he is upheld by an unseen power, and thus the suffering of the believer is a testimoy for his Lord.

III. PERSECUTION GIVES US AN OCCASION TO TRIUMPH OVER IT. — Persecution is the enemy's attempt to triumph over us, but as the great persecution mentioned in the Acts caused the Christians to go everywhere preaching the Word, so persecution, if in the midst of it we trust in the Lord, but acts as the shaking of the thistle, it causes the seed to be scattered, and the thistle is by this means propagated.

1. *Persecution is a triumph when it is for the Lord.* " Blessed are ye when men shall revile you, and persecute you, and shall say all manner of evil against you falsely, for My sake." What an honour to be allowed to do, to be, or to suffer anything for the sake of Christ! One who was persecuted in Queen Mary's time wrote thus: " A poor prisoner for Christ! What is this for a poor worm! Such honour have not all His saints. Both the degrees I took in the university have not set me so high as the honour of becoming the prisoner of the Lord."

2. *Persecution is a triumph when we are persecuted in the Lord.* The Apostle Paul speaks of himself as " the prisoner in the Lord " (Ephes. iv. 1, R.V.). His bonds are due to his union with Christ; hence, as he looks at the marks of suffering on his body, he speaks of them as the " marks of Jesus;" as he remembers that he is chained to the Roman soldier, and kept as a prisoner by the Roman power, he declares that he is the " prisoner of the Lord;" and, as he thinks of all his sufferings, he says that he is filling up the sufferings of Christ for His body's sake which is the Church; hence it is not Paul, but Christ suffering in him. What a difference it would make if we recognised that all our suffering is in the Lord! Then we should see that the darkness but

gives us an opportunity to let our light shine. The storm that sweeps around us gives our Captain occasion to manifest His skill. The dark cloud of tribulation but makes the rainbow of God's grace the more conspicuous. The malice of wicked men is but the dark background that brings out the colours of the graces of the Spirit; and the pit into which men shall thrust us shall but throw us into the hands of those who shall be stepping-stones for our own spiritual advancement, as Joseph's repeated persecutions helped him to reach the goal of prosperity.

"The Jews; who both killed the Lord Jesus and the prophets, and drave out us, and please not God, and are contrary to all men; forbidding us to speak to the Gentiles that they may be saved; to fill up their sins alway: but the wrath is come upon them to the uttermost" (1 Thess. 2:15, 16 R.V.)

17
PERSECUTORS

BY prophecy, by parable, and by statement, the Lord declares that He would be rejected by the Jews, and that punishment would overtake them in consequence. In the prophecies of Isaiah, Zechariah, and Daniel, we are told that Christ would be rejected, cut off, and sold into the hands of wicked men. In the parable of the vineyard and the rejection of the king's son we see the Lord disowned; and in the words, "He came unto His own, and His own received Him not" (John 1: 11), we have the rejection of the Messiah by the Jews. There are two facts seen in the verses before us, namely, the sevenfold description of the sin of the Jews, and the standing evidence of their punishment.

I. THE SEVENFOLD DESCRIPTION OF THE SIN OF THE JEWS.—The trail of the serpent is plainly seen in the enmity of the Jews against Christ and His servants.

1. Killing Lord Jesus. "Killed the Lord Jesus," or as Alford translates the passage, "Killed Jesus the Lord." The burning words of the Apostle

Peter on the day of Pentecost charge the Jews with the same crime, " Him . . . ye have taken, and by wicked hands have crucified and slain " (Acts ii. 23). Again, afterwards he charged them with the same sin, " Ye . . . killed the Prince of Life " (Acts iii. 15). How these cutting utterances of the Apostle remind us of the Psalm where Christ is described as a hind surrounded by bloodhounds (Psalm xxii.), especially those words in it where Christ is made to exclaim, " The assembly of the wicked have enclosed me !"

2. *Murdering the prophets.* " And the prophets." In saying that the Jews had slain the prophets Paul was but echoing the words of Christ when He said, " O Jerusalem, Jerusalem, thou that killest the prophets," &c. (Matt. xxiii. 37). As the Apostle looked along the line of history, and as he glanced through the telescope of prophecy, he saw the red spots that blurred the pages of their record as a nation.

3. *Driving out the Apostles.* " Drave out us." We know from Acts xvii. how they were hunted out from place to place, like murderers being chased by a pack of hungry bloodhounds. In being thus treated they were but having fellowship with their Lord, for He was likewise driven from place to place by the unbelief and persecution of the Jews.

4. *Displeasing to God.* " And please not God." The Jews were habitually pursuing a course that was obnoxious to God, although they were boasting that they were His peculiar people. Saul of Tarsus, in his unconverted state, is an apt illustration of the state of the nation of the Jews, for as he was persecuting Christ in persecuting Christ's people, so

they were displeasing God by their behaviour to His saints.

5. "*Contrary to all men.*" The obstruction of the wicked Jews in preventing the servants of God from preaching the truth of God was most selfish as well as sinful. It was the fable of the dog in the manger illustrated again, for they would not have the truth themselves nor would they let any one else have it. Chrysostom has well said, "If we ought to speak to the world, and they forbid us, they are the common enemies of the world."

6. *Forbidding the Apostles to speak.* The meaning of the word "forbidding" is to "cut short," so that only part of what was intended to be said is uttered. There is abundant proof of this hindering on the part of the Jews as recorded in the Acts of the Apostles, for Paul and his fellow-labourers were expelled from Antioch (Acts xiii. 50); stoned at Lystra (Acts xiv. 19); imprisoned at Philippi (Acts xvi. 24); cried down at Thessalonica (Acts xvii. 5); and hunted out of Berea (Acts xvii. 13).

7. *Filling up their sins.* "To fill up their sins alway." The coming miseries of the Jews are plainly indicated in these words: the destruction of the city of Jerusalem, and their dispersion among the nations; the slaying of myriads of them; and the subjection of many others to slavery and banishment. Because the iniquity of the Amorites was not full in Abraham's time, four hundred years passed away before the promise was fulfilled, in bringing Israel into the land of Canaan; but, as the iniquity of the Amorites increased and filled up their cup, the word of judgment was

fulfilled, and they were dispossessed; even so the Jew was ripening for judgment.

II. THE STANDING EVIDENCE OF THE PUNISHMENT OF THE JEW.—"The wrath is come upon them to the uttermost." If we read "*end*" instead of the word "*uttermost*," for so it is rendered in Matt. xxiv. 6, 13, 14, we shall see that it means that the wrath of God is resting upon the Jewish nation until the end of this dispensation; for, after this, Israel comes into blessing again according to Rom. xi.

What is the lesson for us? It is that God takes note of sin and punishes it. This is true in the history of the nation of Israel; of the sinner; of the Church; and of the individual believer.

1. *This is true in the history of nations.* Take the image mentioned in the book of Daniel, which illustrates the times of the Gentiles, as demonstrating this (Dan. ii.). The head of gold signifies the Babylonian empire; the arms and breast of silver the Medo-Persian kingdom; the thighs and belly of brass portray the Grecian dynasty; and the legs of iron point to the Roman power. As the prophet Daniel saw the times of the Gentiles, they are represented to him (Dan. vii.) as four beasts. From history we know that these nations have been used of God in overthrowing each other in carrying out the Divine judgment, hence the Medo-Persian power overthrows the Babylonian, the Grecians destroy the Medo-Persians, Rome subdues Greece, and the stone cut out of the mountain without hands overthrows all those powers that are represented in the image (Dan. ii. 45 vii. 26-28).

2. *That God punishes sin is seen in the history of the Jews.* Bishop Patrick quotes the following affecting inquiry addressed by Rabbi Samuel Moraccanus to a friend in the eleventh century :—" I would fain learn from thee, out of the testimonies of the law, and the prophets, and other Scriptures, why the Jews are thus smitten in this captivity wherein we are, which may be properly termed the perpetual anger of God, because it hath no end. For it is now above a thousand years since we were carried captive by Titus; and yet our fathers, who worshipped idols, killed the prophets, and cast the law behind their back, were only punished with seventy years' captivity, and then brought home again; but now there is no end of our calamities, nor do the prophets promise any." " If," says Bishop Patrick, " this argument was hard to be answered then in his days, it is much harder in ours, who still see them pursued by God's vengeance, which can be for nothing else but rejecting and crucifying the Messiah, the Saviour of the world."

3. *That God punishes sin is demonstrated in the life of the individual sinner.* Korah· and his followers speak against Moses, and the earth swallows them, and they go down alive into the pit. Aaron's sons bring strange fire into the Lord's presence, and they are dealt with in swift judgment. Achan covets the Babylonish garment and the wedge of gold, things which were consecrated to God, and he is slain for his rebellion.

4. *That God punishes sin is plainly taught in His dealings with the Churches.* The seven Churches of Asia have appeared upon the scene, and they have

passed off the stage, for many of them were not faithful.   The Laodicean Church undoubtedly represents our own time, for it is a picture of the prevailing lukewarmness and looseness that are prevalent everywhere. And Christ says He will spue the whole mass of Christendom out of His mouth, because of the sin which is in it.

5. *That God punishes sin is illustrated in the punishment of the believers at Corinth.*   There were many who had been disobedient in the Church at Corinth, and for this reason God had caused many to be sick, and some had fallen asleep (1 Cor. xi. 30, 32).

From the above briefly stated facts it will be seen that God is watching and noting the actions of men, and that no man can act with impunity.   May we who know the Lord be careful lest we grieve the Holy Spirit in any way, for the Lord will certainly chasten us if we act contrary to His Word.

THE LONGING OF THE
APOSTLE, AND THE
HINDERING OF THE ACCUSER

"But we, brethren, being bereaved of you for a short season, in presence, not in heart, endeavoured the more exceedingly to see your face with great desire : because we would fain have come unto you, I Paul once and again ; and Satan hindered us" (1 Thess. 2:17,18 R.V.)

18

THE LONGING OF THE APOSTLE
AND THE
HINDERING OF THE ACCUSER

IN the above verses we have one of those con-
trasts so marked in the Word of God, namely,
the endeavour of a good man and the fell purpose of an evil spirit in opposing him. The
servant is not above his Master. Christ Himself
was tempted by Satan, who sought to hinder
Him, by the tempting offers of worldly gran-
deur; by the malice of wicked men; by the
suggestion that He performed His miracles by
Satanic agency; by the unfaithfulness of professed disciples; by the unbelief of His Apostles
when they could not cast out the demons; by the
tempest that Satan caused to arise when Christ
was asleep in the boat, thinking to drown the
Son of man in the surging lake; by the betrayal
of Judas; by the denial of Peter; by the false ac-
cusations of wicked men; and by the shame and
ignominy of the cross. Satan sought to hinder
Christ, but Christ kept on His way, and has tri-
umphed over all Satan's power and powers. What
Satan did to Christ, he and his endeavour to do

to us, but it is for us to enter into Christ's victory, and even though our enemy may send some messenger to buffet us, or use wicked men to hinder us, God shall turn the hindrance into a help, and the messenger of Satan into a means of grace, whereby we are able to appreciate the more fully the sufficiency of the grace of God.

I. THE LONGING OF THE APOSTLE.—Paul was no cold stoic, but he was a firebrand alight with the love of God, and was ever alive as a servant of Christ to the need and nurture of those who belonged to Christ. The longing of the Apostle is seen in three ways : in the illustration he uses of a bereaved parent ; in the identification of heart of which he speaks ; and the intensity of desire which he manifested.

1. *The longing of the Apostle is seen in the illustration he uses.* " But we, brethren, being bereaved of you for a short season," &c. The grief of Paul was like that of a father bereaved of his children, or children of their parents. How intensely a mother longs for and thinks of her absent son, who has gone to some distant town. Denney has well said, in commenting on the Apostle's longing:—"There is something wonderfully vivid in the idea which Paul gives of his love for the Thessalonians. His mind is full of them ; he imagines all the circumstances of trial and danger in which they may be placed ; if he could only be with them at need. He seems to follow them as a woman follows with her thoughts the son who has gone alone to a distant town ; she remembers him when he goes out in the morning, pities him if there are any circumstances of hardship

in his work, pictures him busy in shop or office, or street; looks at the clock when he ought to be home for the day; wonders where he is, with what companions in the evening, and counts the days till she will see him again. The Christian love of the Apostle, which had no basis at all in nature, was as real as this, and it is a pattern for all those who try to serve others in the Gospel. The power of the truth, as far as its ministers are concerned, depends on its being spoken in love; unless the heart of the preacher or teacher is really pledged to those to whom he speaks, he cannot expect but to labour in vain."

2. *The longing of the Apostle is seen in the identification of heart of which he speaks.* "Bereaved of you for a short season, in presence, not in heart." "Although we are orphaned of you, for a time, it is not in heart, but in presence." Thus he speaks. There is an electric current that binds believers together which is more vital and lasting in its uniting bond than any tie of nature.

3. *The longing of the Apostle is seen in the intensity of desire he expresses.* "Endeavoured the more exceedingly to see your face with great desire." He uses a word which we have rendered "desire," which means "passion," and often occurs in a bad sense. As a sensualist is consumed by his lusts, so the Apostle longed to see the saints at Thessalonica, that he might minister to them.

II. THE HINDERING OF THE ACCUSER.—How Satan hindered Paul we are not told: whether it was some sin or scandal in the Church at Corinth which made it necessary for him to remain there; whether it was the thorn in the flesh, of which he speaks in another place ; or the attitude of the Jews, who were so bitter against him that he had to flee from Thessalonica, and was chased out of Berea.   Most likely it was the last, as it seems from verse 16.

There are two thoughts upon which we dwell as suggested by the words, " Satan hindered us," and these are, the personality of Satan, and the name by which he is mentioned.

1. *The personality of Satan.*   One of the master moves of Satan in this our day is to get people to believe that there is no such person as the devil. If he can only succeed in this he has accomplished much.   What is the result if the personality of Satan is denied ?   There is a threefold consequence.   The account of the fall of Adam through the suggestion of the devil is a myth, for there was no devil to tempt ; man not being a fallen creature, there is no need for the atonement of Christ ; and therefore there will be no punishment for the sinner.   But we know that Satan is, for we cannot have an effect without a cause.   Who is the author of evil ?   From whence come the crime, the evil, the sin, that are rising on all hands like the inrushing of the tide ?   If there is no devil, from whence comes all the devilishness we see ?   The father of lies is the author of all the business lies that are told, the commercial lies that are circulated, the ecclesiastical lies that are enacted, the literary lies that are printed, and the lies of Christendom that are told in reports of Christian work, in statistics of church membership, and in the professions that are never known in experience.   The god of this

world is the cause of all the boasted agnosticism with its ignorance; the brazen-faced infidelity with its sneers; the prevalent indifferentism with its stupidity; the drunkenness with its crime; the sensuality with its demoralisation; the loftiness of this age with its abominable pride; and the rampant sin with its rebellion against God. But while Satan is the mover and suggester in all these things, he cannot do one single action, nor practise one infamous vice, save as the tempted respond to the temptations of the tempter; hence both shall surely be punished, for both are guilty. This one thing—evil—proves that there is an evil one, and that the trinity of lust—the lust of the flesh, the lust of the eyes, and the pride of life—is begotten by the devil, but is born of the sinner; for, as the devil is the father of sin, so the sinner is the mother of it.

2. *The name which is given to the hinderer,* " Satan." There are two great names by which the enemy of our souls is called, namely, " the devil," which means " the deceiver," and " Satan," which means " the accuser." As the devil, his work is *destructive,* but as Satan, his work is *obstructive.* The very term " hinder" illustrates the obstructive work of Satan. " It is a metaphor taken from military operations—the breaking up of roads, the destroying of bridges, and the interposing of varied obstacles to cut off the enemy's approach or retreat. Or the figure may be that of a racecourse, the up-setting of a chariot by being brought into violent contact with another. Either way, we have a graphic description of the obstructions in the way of the

Apostle's advance. Just as an angel stood in the evil way of Balaam, the apostate prophet, to intercept him, so is Satan here represented as standing in the good way of Paul."

Whenever God is at work Satan is sure to be near to oppose. When Moses performed the miracles as attesting his being sent of God, then Jannes and Jambres appeared upon the scene to withstand him by imitating his wonders by their enchantments. When Nehemiah began to build the wall of Jerusalem, then Sanballat and Tobiah came and threatened to spoil the work.

Satan seeks to hinder by offering to us the things of the world, that he may obtain our homage; as in the case of Christ, when he offered to Him the glory of the kingdoms of this world if He would but worship him (Matt. iv. 9).

Satan tries to obstruct the carrying out of the purpose of God by us, and will even use the Lord's own people for this object if he can; as in the case of Peter, when he rebuked Christ for saying that He must be killed by the elders, and the chief priests, and scribes (Matt. xvi. 22, 23).

Satan hinders the spread of the Gospel, by catching away the Word that is sown in the heart of the stony ground hearer, as Christ says, in the parable of the sower, " Satan cometh immediately, and taketh away the Word that was sown in their hearts " (Mark iv. 15).

Satan hinders the enjoyment of our natural faculties to their full extent, sometimes by marring them with some infirmity, as in the case of the woman who had been bowed together by Satan for eighteen years; and as in the case of the Apostle Paul, who had a thorn in the flesh, the messenger of Satan to buffet him (Luke xiii. 16; 2 Cor. xii. 7). In the former instance the Lord gave deliverance, but in the latter He supplied sufficient grace, so that the Apostle was able to glory in (not merely *bear*) his infirmities that the power of Christ might rest upon him.

Satan hinders by using those who profess to be on the side of Christ, by causing them to take part with those who are against Him; as in the instance of Judas, when Satan entered into him and carried out his unholy purpose in betraying the Lord Jesus for thirty pieces of silver (Luke xxii. 3).

Satan obstructs the growth of the Christian, when through unwatchfulness we place ourselves in his power; as illustrated in the Apostle Peter, when he got him into his sieve through his self-confidence (Luke xxii. 31, 34).

Satan hinders through those who make profession of great things, and tell the Lord that they have done them, when it turns out that they have kept back "part of the price," as when Ananias and Sapphira lied about the possession that they had sold (Acts v. 1, 3).

Satan hinders when he obtains one who has made a profession, but who falls into grievous sin, as in the instance of the fornicator at Corinth, who was delivered by the Church to Satan for the destruction of the flesh (1 Cor. v. 5).

Satan obtains an advantage over us when we act in an unkind and harsh manner towards those who have fallen, but have been restored by the Lord; as when the Church at Corinth were reluctant to receive back the brother to fellowship (whom they had hesitated to put out) when he had repented (2 Cor. ii. 5-7).

Satan hinders when he succeeds in captivating our attention by things that have about them the magical and wonderful, so that our gaze may be diverted from Christ and His Word, as he will do when he causes the Anti-christ, by his Satanic art, to work "signs and lying wonders" (2 Thess. ii. 9).

Satan obstructs when he is able to induce those who once held the faith to give it up, because they have first given up their faith in God and a good conscience; as instanced in Hymenæus and Alexander, who first threw overboard their good conscience, and then ran on the rocks of error, and made, as far as they were concerned, shipwreck of the faith (1 Tim. i. 19, 20, R.V.).

Satan hinders when he can cause any believer to put Christ and His claims second, and not first; as the Apostle says when he speaks of some who were thinking only of marriage and the things of this life in the following words, "Some are turned aside after Satan" (1 Tim. v. 15).

Satan obstructs when he can influence wicked men to persecute the servants of God, by causing them to be driven from any place where the Gospel is being preached; as when the Apostles were chased out of Thessalonica by the wicked Jews.

In conclusion, let us encourage ourselves in the Lord, for, while Satan is a hinderer, he is a usurper, and

Christ has conquered him. Christ has bruised his head; taken away his armour (Luke xi. 22); annulled his power (Heb. ii. 14, R.V.); destroyed his works (1 John iii. 8); spoiled his powers (Col. ii. 15); and taken away the keys of Hades and death, which he once had (Rev. i. 18; Heb. ii. 14). If we fear God we need never fear the devil, for he is a conquered foe. Into Christ's victory let us enter by faith, and in the boldness of the lion of the tribe of Judah we shall be as bold as lions.

" For what is our hope, or joy, or crown of glorying? Are not even ye, before our Lord Jesus at His coming? For ye are our glory and our joy " (1 Thess. 2:19,20)

19

HOPE, JOY AND GLORY

HOW often has one been impressed with the difference between two players upon an organ: the one touches the keys and there is a noise, and a faint indication of the tune; but the other, with a skillful hand, trained ear, and musical sense, makes the instrument speak, and we get melody and music. In like manner, when we come to the beautiful organ of God's Word, we touch the words by meditation, and we have a faint glimmering of the mind of the Spirit; but when the Divine Musician — the Holy Spirit — touches the keys of Divine truth, what heavenly music breaks upon our ear! Our souls are thrilled with delight, our spirits are enraptured, and we are carried out of ourselves as the strains rise and fall in perfect time and wondrous harmony. The skilled musician did not put anything into the organ, but by his skill he brought out what was already there. Even so, in looking at the above Scripture, at first sight all there seems to be is an Apostle's joy over his spiritual children, and the reward he expected when Christ came; and undoubtedly that is the main thought, and the one upon which we shall dwell—but if we put our ear to this shell of Divine utterance we shall hear the murmur of other voices from the great ocean of truth.

For instance, we can see the following things in these verses. (1) There is the fact of Christ's coming, in that the Apostle refers to the time when the saints to whom he was writing would be the reward of all the suffering he had undergone for the sake of the Gospel he loved to preach. (2) In thus referring to the time of Christ's return, and indicating that he would be there and would be known by them and know them, he declares that friends will recognise each other in heaven. (3) The Apostle proclaims that the service of Christ is a means of grace, in saying that those to whom he writes are his joy. (4) Paul speaks of the reward of Christian service in saying that the saints at Thessalonica would be his crown of glorying when he stood before the judgment seat of Christ. These are a few of the precious veins of gold that lie beneath the surface of the verses before us.

There are three words which shall act as steps down into the truth of Paul's utterance, and these are—interrogation, expectation, and affirmation.

I. INTERROGATION.—" For what is our hope, or joy, or crown of glorying?" It may help us to understand this letter if we remember that Paul wrote it from Corinth. He had probably witnessed the Grecian games. Anyway, he knew all about them, for he makes frequent reference to them in illustrating

Divine things, as when he says, " Run the race," and
" We wrestle not against flesh and blood," &c. Now
he seems to say, " As the runner in the race is filled
with the desire and determination to win the prize,
as he strains every power to reach the goal, so, as
I look at you saints, I see that you are not merely
saved, but that you are seeking by all your powers to
be commendable to Christ by obeying His will and
doing His service—thus you are my hope. As the
winner of the prize is filled with joy in that he has
reached the goal first, so I shall be if you who have
been blessed under my ministry have an abundant
entrance into the kingdom of Christ. As the successful
competitor in the games received a crown of laurels,
which was his glory, so I shall receive a crown of
glory when my Lord points to you as those who have
been brought to Himself through me."

1. " *What is our hope?* " The Apostle is not
referring to his own salvation, nor is he thinking of
the safety of those to whom he writes, for they were
delivered from the wrath to come ; but he views them
as his " hope " (trust), in that they will, in spite of
all their difficulties and temptations, be able to rise
above them, so that when Christ comes they will
receive His commendation for having done so, and
thus prove that they were genuine followers of the
Lord Jesus Christ. For, after all, the evidence that
we believe that Jesus died for us is that we died to
all sin, and the proof that we know the living Christ
is that He lives in us and manifests His character
through us. The world can understand the Christ-
like life, as illustrated in the following incident related

by the late C. H. Spurgeon. It was at a church meeting that he reported the death of a young brother, and in doing so he read the following note which he had received from his employer:—"My servant, Edward ——, is dead. I send you word at once, that you may send me another young man; for, if your members are such as he was, I never wish to have better servants around me."

2. "*What is our joy?*" As the Apostle thought of those saints to whom he was writing as the trophies of his toil and conflict it filled him with joy. One has well said, in speaking of the joy that comes through seeking to serve others:—"Here is a high hill, its sides rocky, its surface sterile, its contour uncomely. Nobody wants it or values it. Presently a wise man walks over it, purchases it, cuts away at its sides, and after long and expensive toil lays bare a wealth of precious minerals. So there is many a deed of kindness that waits to be done; yet no one does it. It seems an unpleasant, hard, and costly thing; yet he who at last does it finds in it a treasure." In every kindness there is a joy locked up for your own soul, and the more difficult it is the sweeter the joy. It is sweet to take a loaf of bread to the starving, although it may leave you hungry; to deny oneself of some ornament to clothe the naked; to lose your own sleep to watch beside the suffering. Pearls are found in the unsightly oyster, so pearls of joy are found in tasks from which we shrink. But the sweetest joy is that of saving souls. A man once saved a child's life by snatching it from under the feet of a galloping horse, and ever after that one deed

illumined that man's life. He lay for years in prison cells, but the joys of that heroic hour shone ever in upon his gloom. If it is so blessed to save from physical, how much more to save from eternal death! When Dr. Lyman Beecher was dying some one asked him what was the greatest of all things. He answered, "It is not theology; it is not controversy —it is saving souls."

3. "*What is our crown of glorying?*" This is the highest rung in the ladder. The expression refers to the chaplet of triumph worn by the victor. The same words occur in the Septuagint version of Proverbs xvi. 31, in speaking of an aged righteous person—"The hoary head is a *crown of glory*, if it be found in the way of righteousness." The Apostle uses similar words in other places. For instance, in writing to the Church at Philippi, he says, "My dearly beloved and longed for, my joy, and *crown.*" As the victor boasts of his crown, so the Apostle rejoices in the salvation, sanctification, and service of the converts who had been blessed through his ministry.

II. EXPECTATION.—"Are not even ye before our Lord Jesus at His coming?" There is a great joy in being used of God in the conversion of men, but there is a greater joy when those who profess to have received Christ walk according to the truth. As the mother watches the growth of her child with delight, so the servant of God views with satisfaction the growth of his spiritual children in the grace that is in Christ Jesus; as the sculptor notes the development of the statue while he works at it, so the minister of Christ marks the increase in the spiritual life of one born of God; as the gardener sees the growth of the plants which he has planted, so the husbandman in Divine things notes the graces of the Spirit as they spring up in the life of the child of God; as the artist watches the painting as it is filled in, so the overseer in the Church of God notes with gratification the reproduction of the truth in the life of the disciple of Christ; as the architect sees the building in course of erection, so the builder of the Gospel of Christ beholds with joy the erection of the character that is after Christ.   But the greatest joy of all is when those who are the Lord's finish their course with credit to themselves and honour to their Lord.   It is the full-grown woman that is the pride of the mother; it is the perfect statue that is the ideal of the sculptor; it is the developed plant that the gardener wants; it is the completed picture that is the glory of the artist; and the finished building that stands out to the credit of the architect; even so it is the unsullied life, the pure character, the developed Christian, the faithful steward, and the true servant of Christ that will be the joy and glory of the under-shepherds of the flock of God, when the Chief Shepherd appears to reward them (1 Peter v. 4).

III. *Affirmation.*   "Ye are our joy and glory." " It was the boast of the Jews that to them had been given three crowns—the crown of the law, the crown of the priesthood, and the royal crown.   These they highly prized, but they often added, ' Better than these is the crown of a good name.'   History tells that, when in the reign of Philip the Second a rebel claimed and gained the crown of Granada, he bore at the ceremony of coronation in his right hand a banner bearing the inscription, ' More I could not desire, less would not have contented me.'" Would that every servant of Christ could say of those to whom he ministers, " *More I could not desire,*" in relation to their life and service. Paul could not say of all that they were his joy and glory, but he could say it of those to whom he wrote, for they were patient under tribulation, consistent in life, prayerful in heart, loving in spirit, fruitful in good works, diligent in service, resolute in courage, and desirous of glorifying God.

"Wherefore when we could no longer forbear, we thought it good to be left behind at Athens alone; and sent Timothy, our brother, and God's minister in the Gospel of Christ" (1 Thess. 3:1,2 R.V.)

20
PAUL AT ATHENS

THERE is something very pathetic and stir-
ring in these words of Paul. On the one hand
we have Paul longing to see or to hear of the
young Christians at Thessalonica, as a mother
longs to see or hear of her absent boy; and on
the other hand we have him alone at Athens,
surrounded by idolatry and ignorance, as one
shut off from the fellowship of saints, having
dispatched Timothy to help those disciples of
Christ, in whom he was specially interested. But
we see and admire the unselfishness of Paul in
being willing to remain in solitude for the benefit
of those who were young in the faith, and exposed to the biting wind of tribulation; and we
also behold his love to Christ in thus caring for
the lambs of the flock of God, who were being
harassed by the wolves of the world.

There is some difficulty in this passage as to its
history. Some have thought that it is in conflict
with the account given in Acts 17, but the explanation seems as follows. Paul went from Berea to
Athens (Acts 17: 15), leaving Silas and Timothy

at Berea (Acts xvii. 14). Paul waited at Athens till his fellow-labourers came to him (Acts xvii. 16); and when they came they agreed to send Timothy to Thessalonica to see how the young converts were doing. Meantime Silas goes on another mission not mentioned; hence Paul, in speaking of the sending of Timothy, says, "*We* could no longer forbear;" but in referring to his being at Athens he says, "*I* sent," &c. (verse 5); and he also uses the word "alone," which might be rendered "only," and is so translated in speaking of "the *only* wise God" in 1 Tim. i. 17. Afterwards Silas and Timothy joined Paul at Corinth, where the Apostle had gone, as we gather from Acts xviii. 5; and they there wrote this Epistle to this young Church to encourage and help the members of it.

In pondering the words that express the loneliness of Paul at Athens, and his love towards the saints at Thessalonica, we shall note two things—the love of the Apostle as expressed in his longing after the saints in sending Timothy to them; and his loneliness without his fellow-labourers.

I. THE LOVE OF THE APOSTLE AS EXPRESSED IN HIS LONGING AFTER THE SAINTS IN SENDING TIMOTHY TO THEM.—" We could no longer forbear." The word "forbear" is suggestive. It means to cover up, to conceal, and is used of a water-tight vessel. Paul seems to say, "we kept the longing within ourselves, as a water-tight vessel keeps and conceals the water in it; but at last we could no longer endure the pent-up feeling; we had therefore to let it come out and manifest itself, even as water is let loose from the

place in which it has been confined; and so we sent
Timothy to know how you were progressing in Divine
things." There is a holy solicitude that should mark
all God's saints, in that they should be desirous that
their fellow-saints should be making progress in the
Christian life. How can this be carried out? In
answer to this question we naturally ask another,
viz., What did the early Christians do? We take
three illustrations from the Acts of the Apostles as
showing how we may care for one another, and in
each case we shall see what the Christians did for
each other in sending to them; and as we muse upon
these incidents we shall find that they revolve around
the words *prayer, provision,* and *protection.*

Prayer. In prayer for one another we manifest
our interest in each other. When the Apostles at
Jerusalem heard that Samaria had received the Word
of God, they sent Peter and John down to them, who,
when they came, prayed that they might receive the
Holy Spirit (Acts viii. 14, 15).

In the Apostles' action we have a principle that
should run through our lives, as the electric current
runs along the telegraph wire. If there is one thing
more than another that we need to pray for to-day
it is that the saints may stand perfect and complete
in all the will of God, even as Epaphras prayed for
the Christians at Colosse (Col. iv. 12). We need to
pray that the saints may pray for themselves, that
their hearts may be pure, that their hands may be
clean, that their garments may be unspotted from
the world, and that they may be fully developed in
the Christian life. We need to pray that the disciples

of Christ may sit at the feet of Jesus and learn of Him, as Mary of Bethany, that they may be led into the mysteries of the kingdom; and that they may humbly receive what Christ says without questioning, nor dare to express their opinion or give their views when the utterance of their Lord is plain and pointed. We need to pray that the children of God may take a deep interest in, and have a holy zeal for, the cause of God in holding up the hands and helping with their means those who are proclaiming the whole truth of God.

Provision. When there was a great dearth in the time of Claudius Cæsar we read how the disciples at Antioch determined to relieve the brethren who dwelt in Judea; they gave each one according to his ability, and they sent their contributions by the hands of Barnabas and Paul to the elders for distribution, thus meeting the necessity of the saints and ministering to Christ in serving them. There are some believers who do not know the luxury of giving to the Lord. If there is a bazaar they will buy things that they do not want, because it brings them into prominence. If a collector calls they give because they are asked, not looking into the merits of the appeal, or because their name will appear in the donation list. Oh, to truly give, in seeking out the poor disciples of Jesus! And verily, if done for His sake, He shall say, "For I was an hungered, and ye gave Me meat; I was thirsty, and ye gave Me drink; I was a stranger, and ye took Me in; naked, and ye clothed Me; I was sick, and ye visited Me; I was in prison, and ye came unto Me" (Matt. xxv. 35, 36).

Protection. At one time in the history of the early Church there arose a dissension through certain of the believing Pharisees wanting the Gentile converts to conform to Jewish rites, which necessitated the Apostles and elders to come together and consider the matter. The outcome of the conference was that a letter was sent by the hands of trusted men, which enjoined the Gentile converts to "abstain from meats offered to idols, and from blood, and from things strangled, and from fornication" (Acts xv. 27-29). Thus the young converts were protected from the bondage of Judaism on the one hand, and from the baneful influence of heathenism on the other. Is there not a seam of truth which lies beneath the surface of the action of the Apostles which we may work out? Namely, that we should seek to protect young Christians from religious traditionalism on the one hand, and worldly principles on the other. For instance, do we not find that the mussels and limpets of tradition cling on and sometimes cover the rock of truth; in fact, that forms are put in the place of realities, and the rite of an ordinance covers the reality of it? We need, then, to protect young Christians by telling them of the true meaning and mission of the Church and her ordinances.

II. THE LONELINESS OF THE APOSTLE WITHOUT HIS FELLOW-LABOURERS.—The words of Paul, "left behind at Athens alone," come like the sigh of a disconsolate soul in solitude and sorrow. There is an advantage and also a disadvantage in being shut off from the company of Christians.

There is a disadvantage, for there are certain

risks in being left to oneself.   As one as well said:—
" The self-diabolizing spirit of man always reveals
itself to the lonely contemplatist, either in moments
of vacancy or under the stress of spiritual crises.   Eve
was tempted when she was alone; the suicide suc-
cumbs when he is pushed into the last degree of
loneliness; the darkest thoughts of the conspirator
becloud the mind when he has most deeply cut the
social bond; when man is alone, he loses the check
of comparison with others; he miscalculates his force,
and deems too little of the antagonisms which that
force may excite.   All these are among the risks of
solitude.   The solitary man either degenerates into a
misanthrope and the tool of the diabolizing spirit, or
he enriches and strengthens his life by reverent and
subduing contemplation."

*Again, there is a disadvantage, because the
presence of our brethren tends to help and inspire
us.*   The prudence on our Saviour's part in sending
the disciples out two by two was safe for them, for, if
one was inclined to doubt, the other could stimulate
his faith, and encourage his heart.   There is an incident related of " a monk who could fast seven days in
the monastery.   He tried to do the same thing alone
in the desert.   The effort was too much for him.
He gave out the first day.   'How came you to fail?'
was the question put to him when he returned.
'Ah,' said the monk, ' when I fast in the monastery I
have the prior and the brethren to look on and
encourage me.'"

But solitude has its advantages as well as its disadvantages, and the advantages more than outweigh

the disadvantages. "Think of God working in the solitary things, for the grass does not merely grow around our populous cities, but up there on the side of the bleak Alps, where no traveller has ever passed. Where only the eye of the wild bird has beheld their lovely verdure, the moss and the grass come to perfection, and display all their beauty, for God's works are fair to other eyes than those of mortals. And you, solitary child of God, dwelling far away from any friend, unknown and obscure, in a remote hamlet; or you in the midst of London, hiding away in your little garret, unknown to fame and forsaken by friendship, you are not forgotten by the love of heaven. He maketh the grass to grow all alone, and shall He not make you flourish in loneliness? He can bring forth your graces, and educate you for the skies, in solitude and neglect."

When alone, because driven into solitude by force of circumstances, and we are thus cast upon God, it is an advantage. Jacob found it to be so when he fled from the anger of his brother, and in loneliness was lying upon the stone at Bethel, for then God appeared to him, and assured him that He would be with him and keep him in all his journeyings.

When alone, because driven into exile by persecution, and we hear the voice of God, it is an advantage. Elijah found it so when he was hiding from the rage of Jezebel in the cave at Horeb, although he lamented, "I only am left," for God spoke to him and encouraged him.

When alone, because of the unkindness of kinsfolk, we hide ourselves in isolation, and we meet with God, it is an advantage, as instanced in Moses when God met with him in the mountain and sent him as the deliverer to Israel.

When alone, because, separated from friends, we plead with God that we may serve and please Him, although we are surrounded by those who know not and who love not the Lord, it is an advantage, as to Daniel in Babylon when he prayed to God three times a day, though watched by those who hated him and were jealous of him.

When alone, because the voice of duty calls us to give up some good friend, child, or brother, because the Church of God and the voice of God require it, it is an advantage, as in the case of Paul when he sent Timothy away and was left in isolation at Athens, for anything that is given up, or any act of self-denial, for the sake of God, is always rewarded with His smile and blessing.

RELATIONSHIP—REALM—REASON

"Sent Timothy, our brother and God's minister in the Gospel of Christ, to establish you, and to comfort you concerning your faith" (1 Thess. 3:2 R.V.)

21

RELATIONSHIP—REALM—REASON

TIMOTHY is one of those characters in Scripture which stand out in bold relief, like the buoy which is painted a bright red in the oil painting of the vessel moored in the harbour, so coloured to relieve the sombre appearance of the surroundings. Timothy was as unsullied in his life as the burnished plate which is free from stain; he was as unselfish in his behaviour as the Apostle himself, for Paul has to urge him to take a little wine for his stomach's sake, which, if we read between the lines, tell us that he was fatigued in the Master's service; he was unique in his devotion to Christ as His servant, for Paul speaks of him in the highest terms, not only in this epistle, but also in that to the Church at Corinth; and we may also say that the Apostle had the greatest confidence in Timothy, in that he entrusted him with this important mission to the young Church at Thessalonica.

The words of the text remind us of the Aaronic priesthood. First, the twofold relationship of Timothy as the brother of Paul and Silas, and as the minister of God; just as the priests were the representatives of God and the people.   Secondly, we have *the realm of service,* namely, " in the Gospel of Christ," just as the priests were limited to the service of the tabernacle.   And thirdly, we have *the reason of Timothy's ministry,* which was, that the young Christians to whom he was sent might be established, and comforted concerning their faith, just as the priests were set apart to be a guide and a help to the people of Israel.   Now all God's people are priests, and as such are responsible to be a help and a stimulus to each other.

I.   RELATIONSHIP.—" Timothy, our brother and God's minister."   It will be seen, as we have indicated, that there is a twofold relationship—believerward and Godward.

" Love the brotherhood " is the inspired direction of the Holy Spirit through the Apostle Peter, but there is a brotherhood and a brotherhood.   There is the brotherhood of our common humanity, because of which we should regard with sympathetic concern all mankind; and there is the holy brotherhood of the household of faith, because of which we should love with a peculiar sympathy all believers, as this is the mark of our love of God.   "He that loveth not his brother whom he hath seen, how can he love God whom he hath not seen ?" (1 John iv. 20).   It is in this latter sense that Paul speaks of Timothy as " our brother." In recognising Timothy as his brother Paul indirectly refers to his union with Christ.   For it is our oneness with Christ that makes us one with each other. There are at least two things that are suggested in thinking of our brotherhood in Christ, viz., a common identification with Christ, and a common interest which we should have in each other.

A common identification with Christ. We find the Apostle Paul ringing the changes again and again on those little words " all " and " us " in speaking of the believer's common position in Christ. Is it our relationship as children of God? He says, "Ye are *all* the children of God by faith in Christ Jesus " (Gal. iii. 26), even as the children in the family bear one name and share the same privileges. Is it our oneness with Christ in His death? Then we are told that if " One died for *all*, therefore all died " (2 Cor. v. 15, R.V.), just as the twelve stones that were taken from Gilgal and placed in Jordan represented the whole of Israel. Is it union with Christ in resurrection and in heavenly position? Then the Apostle says to us, as he said to the Church at Ephesus, in speaking of his and their position in Christ, that God hath " quickened *us* together with Christ, . . . and raised *us* up with Him, and made *us* to sit with Him in the heavenly places " (Ephes. ii. 5, 6, R.V.); just as the prince, when he marries a poor girl, not only gives to her his name, but also appoints her to occupy the same position as himself. Is it the indwelling of Christ as the seal that we are God's? Then it is declared that " Christ is all, and in *all* " (Col. iii. 11). It matters not whether we are black or white, old or young, rich or poor, Christ is in *all*. It is the one grace, the grace of God, which saves us all alike; it is the one blood, the blood of Jesus, that cleanses us all from sin; it is the one life, the Spirit of life in Christ Jesus, that has quickened and united, and that lives within us all; it is the one priesthood to which we are all called and set apart for holy service and worship; it is the one Book, the Word of God, which is the basis of our faith; it is the one home, the house of God, to which we are all travelling; it is the one family to which we belong.   Hence we are brethren, and as such occupy the like position, just as the names of the children of Israel, according to their birth, were engraven on the onyx stones which were on the shoulders of the high priest, who was the representative of Israel; thus they were all identified with him.

A common interest in each other.   As the branches of the vine are united to each other, because of their oneness in the vine; as the members in the body are united the one to the other, because of their union with the head; as the brothers in business are identified with their father as partners in the firm— even so the believer shares a common position with all believers, and, because of this, there should be a common interest in each other.   There is one phrase which the Apostle uses in speaking of our union with Christ as the ground of our oneness with each other and the unity that should be dominant in consequence, and that is as follows, " which every joint supplieth." The whole verse reads, " From whom the whole body fitly joined together, and compacted by that which every joint supplieth, according to the effectual work- ing in the measure of every part, maketh increase of the body unto the edifying of itself in love " (Eph. iv. 16).   As every joint in the body is dependent the one upon the other, so every member in the mystical

body of Christ ministers the one to the other. It is
not the one or the few flakes of snow that make the
glacier, but it is the consolidated frozen mass of snow
that constitutes it; even so, all who believe in Christ
make up the holy brotherhood of the household of
faith. And as such they should serve one another in
holy service, as the Lord said when He washed the
disciples' feet; they should suffer with each other in
the hour of affliction and trial, even as the Son of God
was with the three young men in the fiery furnace;
and succour one another in the time of need, even
as Onesiphorus did the Apostle Paul when he was in
prison (2 Tim. i. 16).

Reference is not only made to Timothy as a
"brother," but he is also spoken of as "God's minister,"
which denotes his relationship *Godward*, as an
instrument which God used in His service, for doubt-
less the more correct reading is as the Revised
Version puts it, viz., "And God's minister in the
Gospel," not as the Authorised Version, "and minister
of God, and our fellow-labourer in the Gospel."
Christian service may be viewed from *four different
standpoints*.

As *stewards* we occupy *for* Christ in obedience to
His directions; as *slaves* we are *under* the Lord, as
such to do His bidding; as *partners* we are yoked
with Christ, as having fellowship with Him by being in
communion with Him while serving; and as *instruments* we are used *by* God, as the workman uses the
tool as he wills. The last illustration is what is
meant by the Apostle when he speaks of Timothy as
being God's minister. It is not the brush that paints

the splendid water colour, but the skill of the artist in using the brush; it is not the chisel that makes the beautiful statue, but the sculptor's use of the chisel; it is not the hydraulic power that fills the organ with wind that brings out the modulated sounds from the organ, but the touch and manipulation of the organist; and it is not the Christian worker who can render effective service, but it is God who uses him, who works the service that is beneficial, and who makes the believer a blessing.

II. REALM.—"In the Gospel of Christ." "*In Christ*" is the sphere of the believer's standing and satisfaction; "*in the Lord*" is the environment of the Christian's responsibility and rejoicing; "*in love*" is the atmosphere in which the saint is to live, that he may love as Christ loves; "*in the truth*" is the circle in which the child of God is to walk, that he may expound and emphasize the Word of God; "*in the Spirit*" is the region to which we are separated that we may know His power and be used by Him in His service; and "*in the Gospel*" is the realm to which we are limited in the ministry to which God calls us. We may not descend to the lower plane of social reform, lop off the branches of iniquity, and leave the tree and roots of sin untouched. We may not come down to the lower world of mere morality, which but burnishes the outside of the man and leaves untouched the heart of uncleanliness within. Let the conscience be cleansed from guilt by the blood of Christ, and the heart purified by the presence of Christ, and there must follow the clean hands of the righteous action, and the clean life of honesty and holiness. If we truly minister the Gospel, it will be apprehended that the death of Christ, which is the key that unlocks and opens the door of salvation that we may enter in, is also the door of separation that shuts us in with God as Noah in the ark, and thus away from the servitude of sin and the slavery of the world.

Let us serve in the Gospel of Christ, for it is the *medicine* that can alone heal broken hearts and minister deliverance to the conscience burdened by sin. The Gospel is the *magnet* to draw the sinner away from the love of sin and from the desire to sin. The Gospel is the *mould* that shall fashion the life of the sinner anew, so that old things shall pass away and all things shall become new, under the controlling power of the living and indwelling presence of Christ.

III. REASON.—The reason of Timothy's mission was, as the following words declare, " to establish and comfort you concerning your faith." There are three things that will make us steadfast and sure in regard to our faith, which every true-hearted believer should seek to have for himself and others—then there will be mutual comfort and stability—and these are, an unveiled face before God, unwavering faith in God's Word, and unceasing fidelity in God's work.

1. *An unveiled face before God.* As the uncovered mirror reflects the image of the person who is looking into it, so, as there is no veil of worldliness, or pride, or selfishness, or covetousness, or cowardice, shall Christ be seen in the life. Many lament their want

of stability when they should confess their sin in want of thoroughness to Christ.

2. *An unwavering faith in God's Word.* "There are two things that have kept me right," said one Christian to another recently, "and these are: I believe, not in something about Christ, but in Christ Himself; and the Bible to me is more than a book: it is the voice of the living God." When the Bible is God's voice to the man there will be no questioning as to its authority, but whole-hearted obedience to its commands.

3. *An unceasing fidelity in God's work.* There are some professors who are always bemoaning their leanness, whereas they should be confessing to their laziness Others, again, think that they have a special vocation in finding fault with those who are at work. And yet another class are subject to "fit-and-startism." If there are special meetings they are most prominent. If some special friend comes and gives an address they are to the front; but as to plodding and diligence in Christian work they are lacking. If we are working for God, we shall regard neither the approval nor the disapproval of either friends or foes, but shall persistently continue in well-doing.

GOOD TIDINGS

"That no man be moved by these afflictions; for yourselves know that hereunto we are appointed. For verily, when we were with you, we told you beforehand that we are to suffer affliction ; even as it came to pass, and ye know. For this cause I also, when I could no longer forbear, sent that I might know your faith, lest by any means the tempter had tempted you, and our labour should be in vain. But when Timothy came even now unto us from you, and brought us glad tidings of your faith and love, and that ye have good remembrance of us always, longing to see us, even as we also to see you," &c. (1 Thess. 3:3-6 R.V.)

22
GOOD TIDINGS

MANY of the subjects mentioned in the above verses have already come under our review in pondering this Epistle: such matters as the afflictions of the saints, the desire of the Apostle Paul to see the disciples who were severed from him, his loving interest in these believers in sending Timothy to them, and the evil purpose of Satan to tempt them to forsake the Lord. We need not, therefore, traverse the ground again, although there might be other aspects of the subjects than those already given. We shall rather direct attention to the good tidings that Timothy brought to the Apostle from and about those to whom he had sent him.

The good tidings. "As cold waters to a thirsty soul, so is good news from a far country" (Prov. 25:25). Next to the good tidings of great joy of a Saviour who comes to act for us, is for the Saviour's work in the believer to be manifest in the steadfastness of faith in Christ and sterling love to Him which give unspeakable joy to the servant of Christ who is in fellowship with Him.   We can imagine with what intensity Paul waited for Timothy's return, and his abounding joy as he listened to Timothy's recital of the healthiness of the faith of those at Thessalonica, the harmoniousness of their love, and their hearty appreciation of himself in that they reciprocated his desire to see them.   It will be seen that there are three items in the verbal budget of Timothy's message, viz., faith, love, and remembrance, which may be summed up as healthy faith, harmonious love, and hearty appreciation.

I. HEALTHY FAITH.—If this Epistle to the Thessalonians is read through carefully, it will be seen that in it "faith" occupies a very important place, yea, we might almost say the chief position among the graces of God, for faith is the door that leads to all the rest.   We briefly note the different colours in the garment of faith as seen in this Epistle.

1. The work of faith (i. 3).
2. The imitation of faith (i. 7).
3. The witness of faith (i. 8).
4. The reliability of faith (ii. 4).
5. The encouragement of faith (ii. 10).
6. The power of faith (ii. 13).
7. The helping of faith (iii. 2).
8. The knowledge of faith (iii. 5).
9. The fellowship of faith (iii. 6).
10. The comfort of faith (iii. 7).
11. The growth of faith (iii. 10).
12. The object of faith (iv. 14).
13. The protection of faith (v. 8).

Faith is the creeper that clings to and lives upon

Christ, as the ivy adheres to the oak, and lives upon it. Alleine has well said, in speaking of the marks of a believer, "A true Christian is like a vine that cannot stand of itself, but is wholly supported by the prop it leans upon. A true believer is like a glass without a foot, set him where you will he is ready to fall every way till you set him to a prop." And we may add, that as the ivy is nourished and upheld as it clings to the oak and sends its roots into it, so the Christian is upheld and nourished as he cleaves to the Lord with full purpose of heart. In the ivy living upon the oak there are two things that are suggested, namely, isolation and impregnation. *Isolation.* As the creeper climbs up the trunk of the tree, it is separated from the under-growth of the wood, and is able to get the full benefit of the air and the sun. In like manner, as we cleave to Christ in trustful obedience to His word, we are separated from the evil of sin and the world around us and lifted up into the clear atmosphere of God's presence, and into the warm sunlight of His love. *Impregnation.* The ivy by its clinging to the oak draws from it the life that is in it, and thus the ivy is impregnated with the life that is in the oak; even so as we live upon Christ through whole-hearted response to His commands, and prayerful meditation on His words, we partake of His life. Thus in His life, we live; in His love, we love; in His strength, we are strong; in His holiness, we are holy; in His humility, we are humble; in His compassion, we are compassionate; in His devotion, we are devoted; and in His prayerfulness, we pray.

Faith is the cable that connects the soul and Christ, and thus keeps the believer steady amid the difficulties of life. The eternal God, in all the perfection of His love and grace, and in all the power of His holiness and justice, is the sure anchorage ground of the believing heart. Christ in the completeness of His death and resurrection for us, and in the comeliness of His person, is our Anchor; the faith of the believer is the Spirit-made cable which can never break as long as we trust in Christ, and the Holy Spirit is the One who fixes the link of committal to Christ on the soul end of the cable to the indestructible vessel of God's eternal truth, and who also connects the link of consecration to Christ on the Christ end of the cable to His living Person. Thus connected and fixed, and thus anchored, who can move us? None, as long as faith in Christ remains. We need to be careful that the rust of worldliness does not eat its way through any link of our life, for if it does we shall be like those of whom Paul speaks who made shipwreck of faith and of a good conscience (1 Tim. i. 19, 20). Many a one has seemed to start well, but, as depicted in the thorny-ground hearer, he has allowed things of the world to come in and corrupt him. A well-known preacher relates the following incident, which shows the cause and consequence of the rust of worldliness eating through the link of professed faith in Christ. "I had a friend who started in commercial life as a book merchant, with a high resolve. He said, ' In my store there shall be no books that I would not have my family read.' Time passed on, and one day I went into his store and found some iniquitous books on the shelf, and I said to him, 'How is it possible that you can consent to sell such books as these?' 'Oh,' he replied, 'I have got over those puritanical notions. A man cannot do business in this day unless he does it in the way other people do it.' To make a long story short, he lost his hope of heaven, and in a little while he lost his morality, and then he went into a madhouse." In other words, "when a man casts off God, God casts him off."

Faith is the cement that consolidates us, so that we are unmoved by the afflictions that beat upon us. The word translated "moved" (in verse 3) is used of dogs *wagging* their tails in fawning on one. The Apostle desired that the faith of the saints to whom he sent Timothy should be the opposite to that of a fawning dog, whose tail moves to and fro as indicating that it is influenced by your manner towards it. Paul found that those to whom he sent were what he desired, for the messenger's report is that their faith is fixed and firm. Their faith is an adhering and adhesive power which unites them and Christ in an indissoluble bond, for as the cement unites the stones together, so faith binds Christ and the believer. The storms may howl about the Eddystone lighthouse, and the waves beat and lash about it as if to engulf it and end its beneficent mission, but because it is built into and united to the rock bed beneath, as the roots of the oak in the earth, it stands unmoved. Fellow-Christian, the winds of temptation will blow upon you, but remember Christ is for you; as Satan raised the storm on the lake when Christ was asleep in the boat to drown Him and His disciples, so he will seek to overthrow you, but remember that He who calmed the storm on the lake of Gennesaret can give you deliverance.

Tried believer, the billows of affliction will come rolling towards you like the mountainous waves of the Atlantic, and they may seem as if they were going to overwhelm you, but trust in Christ, and He shall cause your bark to surmount all the angry seas; thus you shall find that " tribulation worketh patience; and patience, experience; and experience, hope; and hope maketh not ashamed; because the love of God is shed abroad in our hearts by the Holy Ghost, which is given unto us " (Rom. v. 3-5). Persecuted child of God, the storm of ridicule, of sneers, and it may even be of angry words and blows, shall beat upon you, but trust in the Lord, and He shall keep you calm and patient; thus like your Saviour you shall be, for " when He was reviled, He reviled not again " (1 Peter ii. 23).

> " Oh trust thyself to Jesus !
>   When tempted to transgress
> By hasty words or angry look,
>   Or thought of bitterness.
> Then is the hour for claiming
>   Thy Lord to fight for thee ;
> Then is the time for singing,
>   ' He doth deliver me.' "

II. HARMONIOUS LOVE.—Timothy not only brought good tidings of the faith of the Christians, but also a glad report about their love. Harmonious love is a triangle. Upon one side, pointing upwards, we read, " Love *to* Christ ;" upon the other side, pointing downwards, we see, " Love *as* Christ ;" and along the bottom is written, " Love *for* Christ. "

Love to Christ. To love Christ we must know Christ's love to us; as John says, " We love Him, because He first loved us." It is Christ's love to us, in bearing the cross for us, that makes us willing to bear the cross and follow Him. It is Christ's love to us in dying for our sins on the accursed tree that constrains us to die to sin. It is Christ's love to us in rising from the dead, and revealing Himself as the living, ascended, and glorified One, that is the magnet to draw us after Him to live in God's will and for His glory. It is Christ's love to us in working out our salvation, by finishing the task that the Father gave Him to do, that is the inspiring motive that causes us to work out our salvation by adding to our faith what the Lord enjoins (2 Peter i.). It is Christ's love to us in suffering the agonies of Gethsemane and Calvary that enables us to suffer for and with Him. It is Christ's love to us in dying on our behalf that calls us to be willing to lay down our lives for the brethren. And it is Christ's love to us in rescuing us from the power of sin and Satan that directs us to rescue others from the power of Satan and the slavery of sin. May we show our love to Christ at all times.

It is related of an old gentleman that he had a weather vane put upon his premises, and on the vane he had the words " God is love." Some one found fault with him for putting the words " God is love " upon the vane, remarking " that the love of God was not a fickle thing like the wind." The old man replied that "what he meant was, no matter which way the wind blew, God was love." In like manner the weather vane of our life should ever speak of love to Christ, no matter how fiercely the storms of temptation may howl around us or the tempests of persecution may assail us.

Love as Christ. The law demanded that man should love his neighbour as himself, but Christ enjoins us to love each other as He has loved us (John xv. 12). Remember how *expensively* He loved us. It was Himself He gave. Let the manger with its humble surroundings, let the mountain side with the pleading Saviour, let the poverty of Christ's life, let the agony of Gethsemane, the scourging of Gabbatha, the scoffing of Golgotha, the shame of the cross, the forsaking on Calvary, and His death for us, tell out how expensively He loved us, and what it cost Him to make us His own. Ponder how *expressively* He loved us. He saw us in our sins unlovely and unloving, as Ezekiel's infant (Ezek. xvi. 6, 12), cast out in the open field of condemnation, covered with the blood of iniquity, helplessly in the bondage of sin, and exposed to the righteous anger of God; then it was that He cleansed us from our pollution, covered us in His righteousness, decked us with the graces of the Spirit, shod us with the shoes of peace, and made us beautiful in His comeliness. Meditate how *extensively* He loved us. As our Kinsman He became one with us, as our Sacrifice He bled for us, as our Prophet He taught us, as our Redeemer He delivered us, as our Avenger He fought for us, as our Propitiation He met God's claim for us, and as our

Refuge He hides us. It is as we see Christ's love
to us in the manner of its operation that we are able
to imitate Him in dealing with others, and it is as
the love of Christ constrains and fills us that we are
able to love as He loved and loves, for as water rises
to its own level, so, as the love of Christ dwells in us,
we shall in our measure be able to rise to the level of
loving others as He loved us.

Love for Christ. "Love *to* Christ" points upwards
to Him who is the Object of our affection; "love *as*
Christ" directs us towards our fellow-believers, to act
towards them as our Lord acted, in relation to ourselves; and "love *for* Christ" leads us to look towards
the world, to those who are in sin and walking after
the course of this evil age. It is for Christ's sake
that we go in obedience to His command with the
message of His Gospel. It is for Christ's sake that
we are willing to become fools, and be counted as the
offscouring of society. It is for Christ's sake that we
are willing to become all things to all men, that we
may gain some of them for Him.

III. HEARTY APPRECIATION.—"That ye have good
remembrance of us always, longing to see us, even as
we also to see you." The believers to whom Paul
was writing were as desirous to see him as he was to
see them. They thus showed their appreciation of
this honoured and beloved servant of Christ.

"Therefore, brethren, we were comforted over you, in all our affliction and distress, by your faith : for now we live, if ye stand fast in the Lord" (1 Thess. 3:7,8 A.V.)

23

STEADFASTNESS
AND
ITS INFLUENCE UPON OTHERS

THE "ifs" of Holy Writ are like the provisoes in an agreement; they imply conditions to be fulfilled, and terms to be met. Our Lord often puts in an "if" in His sayings, which are like so many landmarks to indicate the right path. There is the "if" of the denial of self if we would follow Christ: — "If any man will come after Me, let him deny himself, and take up his cross daily, and follow Me" (Luke 9:23). There is the "if" of thoroughness and its reward: — "If thy whole body therefore be full of light, having no part dark, the whole shall be full of light" (Luke 11: 36). There is the "if" of true discipleship:— "If ye continue in My word, then are ye My disciples indeed" (John 8: 31). There is the "if" of the honour of service: — "If any man serve Me, him will My Father honour" (John 12: 26). There is the "if" of happiness: — "If ye know these things, happy are ye if ye do them" John 13: 17). These words Christ uttered to tell His disciples to wash one another's feet. There is the "if" of obedience as the expression of love to Christ: — "If ye love Me, keep My commandments"

(John xiv. 15). There is the "*if*" *of answered prayer* which is consequent upon our abiding in Christ and His words abiding in us:—"*If* ye abide in Me, and My words abide in you, ye shall ask what ye will, and it shall be done unto you" (John xv. 7). And in the text we have the "*if*" *of communicated life*, for undoubtedly the sense in which the words occur is, that the steadfastness of the saints was to Paul and his companions as a cordial to revive them. From this we learn how powerfully our lives influence others either for good or evil.

There are two things suggested by the words of the text, viz., steadfastness, and its influence upon others.

I. STEADFASTNESS.—There are eight or nine places in the New Testament where the words "stand fast," or their equivalent, occur. As the petals in the flower have a similarity, and yet each one is distinct, so the Scriptures where we are exhorted to "stand fast" have a definite application, and yet they are all connected with the subject of steadfastness, and illustrate it in its different bearings.

1. *Steadfastness in the faith.* "Stand fast in the faith" (1 Cor. xvi. 13). "The faith" spoken of is what is believed, and not the act of believing. As the woman in the parable had three measures of meal, so there are three parts in the faith of the Gospel, which are summed up as follows:—

THE WORD OF THE FATHER.
THE WORTH OF THE SON.
THE WORK OF THE SPIRIT.

Therefore "The faith" is a trinity. In like manner,

each part of the faith is triune. The Word of the Father was communicated to Christ, which He as the Faithful Witness and Apostle delivered to us. The Word of the Father was lived out and is expressed in the life of Christ, as the Divine Logos, so that all that He was and did are the manifestation of the Word of God. And the Word of God is received by the believer, whom it quickens, and in whom it shows its presence by his prompt, willing, and loving obedience. The *worth of the Son* is seen in three particulars. There is His worth as the Eternal Son of God, as the One perfectly qualified to act on our behalf, so that His action is the action of God. There is His worth as the Sacrifice for sin, for He alone could effectually and efficiently take up, deal with, and for ever settle the question of sin, and this He has done by the sacrifice of Himself. And there is the worthiness of Christ as the Son of man, as demonstrated in that the Father has crowned Him with glory and honour, and hath committed all judgment into His hands. The *work of the Spirit* is also threefold. There is His work in salvation in quickening us from the death of sin; there is His operation in sanctification, in enabling us to be dead to sin, and alive unto God in holiness of heart and righteousness of life; and there is His use of us as He takes us up and makes us His instruments in His service.

Now let any believer stand fast in this faith, and he shall be like a house built upon a rock. When the winds of temptation, the storms of sin, and the hailstones of error come, he shall be safe and steady, and weather the hurricane.

2. *Steadfastness in the liberty of the Gospel.*
" Stand fast therefore in the liberty wherewith Christ
hath made us free " (Gal. v. 1). The saints at
Galatia were in danger of going back to the cere-
monialism of the law, and thus placing themselves
under the system which demanded perfection in all
its performances, but gave no power to carry them
out. Now the Gospel not only demands, but gives
what it requires. The Gospel does not tell us to be
occupied with rites and ceremonies. A clean life is
of more importance than the washing of hands. A
clean heart is before mere outward observances. To
stand fast in the liberty of the Gospel is to be in the
clear sunlight and warmth of God's love, and to have
that love as the inspiring motive in all our actions.

3. *Steadfastness in conflict by having on the
armour of God.* " Put on the whole armour of God,
that ye may be able to stand against the wiles of the
devil" (Eph. vi. 11). We have three great enemies:—
the flesh, which we are to *ignore ;* the world, which
we are to *avoid;* and the devil, whom we are to *resist.*
Now to be able to do this we must have on the whole
panoply of God. But having on the armour of God
we shall be able to stand against him. The only
thing about which we must be careful is to have on
the *whole* armour of God, for if we are wanting in
one part Satan will be sure to find it out, and lay us
low in defeat. Christ is our whole armour, therefore
let us " put on the Lord Jesus Christ, and make not
provision for the flesh, to fulfil the lusts thereof."
Christ as the Wisdom of God is our Helmet; Christ
as the Righteousness of God is our Breastplate; Christ

as the Refuge of God is our Shield; Christ as the
Truth of God is our Girdle; Christ as the Peace of
God is our Protection; and Christ as the Word of
God is our Sword.

4. *Steadfastness in unity.* "Stand fast in one
spirit" (Philip. i. 27). What is it that has given our
British soldiers the victory again and again when
they have been pressed by overwhelming numbers on
the battlefield? It is the impregnable squares that
they have formed, so that from whatever point the
enemy has come they have been met with a steady
and a deadly fire. If the enemy could only break the
square, then there would be confusion and defeat at
once. Let us be drilled by the Holy Spirit to form
this holy square of oneness of spirit, and keep it by
prayerful watching. The secret of the early Church's
prosperity is given us again and again in the Acts of
the Apostles in those words, "One accord," which
come like the strains from a well-tuned instrument
in musical harmony as it is being played by a skilled
musician.

5. *Steadfastness in the Lord.* "So stand fast in
the Lord" (Philip. iv. 1). There is a reason for standing fast in the Lord, and that is found in the third
chapter, twentieth and twenty-first verses. What
was the reason for Abram's leaving his native land,
and becoming a pilgrim and a stranger on the earth?
It was because God had called him to a higher
and a better inheritance. In like manner the believer
belongs to heaven. His inheritance is there, and he
is looking for the return of the Lord Jesus. The
reason why the Christian has nothing in common

with the world is because he has been separated from it by the Lord Himself.

6. *Steadfastness in the will of God.* "Stand perfect and complete in all the will of God" (Col. iv. 12). Epaphras prayed that the saints at Colosse might stand perfect in all the will of God, that is, that they might fully answer to the end for which they were saved, for so the word "perfect" means, as we may gather from Heb. v. 14, where the term is translated "full age," and 1 Cor. xiv. 20, where it is translated "men." God's will is that we should be complete and stand firm in His will.

7. *Steadfastness in the truth.* "Stand fast, and hold the traditions" (2 Thess. ii. 15). The Gospels reveal to us Christ in the perfection of His life, and the end of that life in His sacrificial death; the Revelation unfolds to us the things that are to take place after Christ's people are taken away at His second coming; and the Epistles draw aside the veil, and give us to look into the glory, and there to see what Christ is now doing for us. It is the Epistles to which the Apostle refers when he speaks of "the traditions," for they specially unfold to us the glorified Person of Christ, and the dignified position of the Christian, as being "in Christ." We may apply his words to ourselves as follows :—Let us stand fast in Christ as our Justification by an ever-present faith in Him, as brought out in the Epistle to the Romans. Let us stand fast in Christ as our Sanctification, by being always separate to Him, as stated in the Epistles to the Corinthians. Let us stand fast in Christ as our Liberator, by abiding in Him, as enforced in Galatians.

Let us stand fast in Christ as our Power, by allowing Him to dwell in our hearts, as prayed in Ephesians. Let us stand fast in Christ as our Satisfier, by rejoicing in Him, as exhorted in Philippians. Let us stand fast in Christ as our Head, by being subject to Him, as commanded in Colossians. Let us stand fast in Christ as our High Priest, by placing all our affairs in His hands, as directed in Hebrews; and let us stand fast in Christ as our Lover, by loving Him as manifest in a life of obedience, as pointed out in the Epistles of John.

8. *Steadfastness in the grace of God.* " The true grace of God: stand fast therein " (1 Peter v. 12, R.V.). As the breath makes the indentations in the wax cylinder of the phonograph, which cause the words to be reproduced, so as we stand fast in the grace of God we shall be humble in heart, thankful in spirit, careful in walk, watchful in action, prayerful in thought, hearty in love, and graceful in manner. It is said that there is a marine plant which rises from a depth of a hundred and fifty to two hundred feet, and floats on the surface of the water, in the midst of the great breakers of the Western Ocean. The stem of this plant is less than an inch through; yet it grows and thrives and holds its own against the fierce smitings and pressures of the breakers, which no masses of rocks, however hard, could withstand. What is the secret of this marvellous resistance and endurance ? It reaches down into the still depths, where it fixes its grasp, after the fashion of the instinct that has been put into it, to the naked rocks, and no commotion of the upper water can shake it

loose.   In like manner as we grasp by a living faith and abide in the grace of God, we shall be as immovable as the Eternal Rock of Ages.

II. THE INFLUENCE WE EXERT UPON OTHERS IF WE ARE STEADFAST.—"*We* live," says the Apostle, in speaking of himself and his fellow-helpers, "if *ye* stand fast."   Mark the "we" and "ye," for it tells us that the Apostles were *dependent* in their progress in Christian life; they "lived" as the young Christians to whom they were writing were steadfast.   This may be apprehended at once if we call to mind that we are members one of another, and therefore none of us live unto ourselves.   We are either influencing others for good or ill.   Our every action tells.   Dr. Macmillan says,—"Chemists tell us of substances whose passiveness is disturbed by the slightest motion, so that they rush into permanent combinations.   The touch of a feather will cause the iodine of nitrogen to explode, and the vibration of any kind of sound will decompose it.   The scratch of a pin will so alter the arrangement of the molecules of iodine of mercury that their action on light is altered, and the colour of the whole mass is changed at once from yellow to bright red.   Many other substances could be named whose equilibrium is so unstable, whose affinity is so weak, that the most insignificant and apparently inadequate causes will immediately change their properties, so that they become henceforth quite different from what they were before.   It is because the equilibrium of the substance on which he operates is so unsteady that the photographer produces his permanent pictures by sunlight; and the greater the instability or sensitiveness of the collodion, the shorter the time required to make the impression, and the deeper and more lasting it will be. Among the high Alps, early in the year, the traveller is told in certain places to proceed as quietly as possible. On the steep slopes overhead, the snow hangs so evenly balanced that the sound of the voice, the crack of a whip, the report of a gun, or the detachment of a snowball, may destroy the equilibrium, and bring down an immense avalanche that will overwhelm everything within reach in ruin. Applying these illustrations of the physical world to the condition of society around us, are there not many whose moral character is so unstable, whose principles are so un-fixed, who are so evenly balanced between good and evil, that a word, a look, may incline them to the one side or the other, and produce effects that will alter the colour and the nature of their whole future exis-tence ? Are there not souls around us hanging so nicely poised on the giddy slopes of temptation, watching us, and ready, on the least encouragement to evil from us—of which we ourselves are not con-scious—to come down in terrible avalanches of moral ruin, crushing themselves and others in their fall ? Are there not earnest ones whose holier purposes may have been quenched for ever by our levity and impropriety of conduct ?"

And may we not add—if we as believers are truly pungent in holiness of life as the salt of the earth, and really shining in the compassion of love as the light of the world, we shall exert an influence that shall be widespread in its mission.

" For what thanksgiving can we render again unto God for you, for all the joy wherewith we joy for your sakes before our God ; night and day praying exceedingly that we may see your face, and may perfect that which is lacking in your faith ?" (**1 Thess. 3:9,10 R.V.**)

24

A HOLY SQUARE

THE verses that form the basis of our meditation are like the altar of burnt-offering, they are
four-square. Upon one side we read the word
"thankfulness;" upon another, "joy;" upon another, "prayer;" and upon the other, "faith."
The first and the third of these are like the
ascending angels on Jacob's ladder — they go
upward to the throne of God; and the second and
fourth are like the descending angels—they come
downward to us. Thanksgiving is the grace that
goes to God with hands filled with the sacrifice of
praise. Joy is the development of the Spirit-
implanted life, as the fruit is the superabundance
of life in the tree. Prayer is the uprising of the
soul as stirred by the Holy Spirit, as the volcano
is the outcome of fires within the earth. Faith
is a heaven-born plant, that needs a favourable
environment for its growth.

I. THANKFULNESS.—"For what thanksgiving can
we render again unto God for you?" Paul had giv-
en thanks for the conversion of those to whom he

wrote (i. 2); he had given thanks for the manner in which they had received the Word (ii. 12); and now he would offer thanksgiving for their steadfastness and sanctity, but he knows not how much thanksgiving to render, as he is so overpowered with the ring of their testimony and the reality of their faith. We all know something of this experience, when we are so overcome with gratitude that we cannot give expression to what we feel.

As we look beneath the surface of this heart interrogation we can see that the Apostle recognized that all that the saints were was of God, and therefore all the praise was due to Him. It is said that Telford stated to a friend, only a few months before his death, that for some time previous to the opening of the Menai Suspension Bridge his anxiety was so great that he could scarcely sleep, and that a continuance of that condition must have very soon completely undermined his health. We are not surprised, therefore, to find that when his friends rushed to congratulate him on the result of the first day's experiment, which decisively proved the strength and solidity of the bridge, they should have found the engineer on his knees engaged in prayer. A vast load had been taken off his mind : the perilous enterprise of the day had been accomplished without loss of life ; and his spontaneous act was thankfulness. In like manner, as the Apostle viewed the result of the work that God had begun through him he was filled with gratitude to God for its stability and success.

As the beautiful bouquet of sweet scented flowers

fills the room with its fragrance, and so reminds us
of the kind thoughtfulness of the friend who brought
them, so thanksgiving to God shows that we
remember His mercies, and that we are grateful to
Him for them. As the cup of cool spring water
refreshes the weary traveller who has been walking
beneath the scorching sun, so the grateful heart
refreshes God, and causes Him to behold the thankful
one with the smile of complacency. As the sacrifice
of the burnt-offering went up to God as a sweet
smelling savour, so the sacrifice of thanksgiving
perfumed with the name of Jesus is a delight to
Jehovah. Let us by all means praise Him for what
He does for us individually, but let us also thank
Him when we see others who are steadfast and true
to Him.

II. JOY.—" For all the joy wherewith we joy for
your sakes before our God." In verse seventh we
read that Paul and his fellow-labours had been
" comforted " by the faith of the saints at Thessalonica ; and now they rejoiced in the Lord for all that
they were and did. That joy was pure and unselfish ;
and it was in the Lord's presence, therefore it met
with His approval. It is a good thing to rejoice over
others, and that for three reasons—for our own sake,
for others' sake, and for the Lord's sake.

1. We should rejoice in what the Lord does for
others, *for our own sake.* As he who digs a pit for
another is sure to fall into it himself sooner or later,
so the one who rejoices in what the Lord does for
others brings a blessing upon himself. There is too
much of the spirit of the elder son in the parable of

the prodigal among us. The elder brother is depicted as grumbling instead of rejoicing at the return of his brother, which brought a gentle rebuke from his father, and revealed a bad state of soul in himself. Let us be careful that the green-eyed monster of jealousy has no place in our hearts; but let the expulsive power of Christ's love fill us, then all that is unkind shall be kept out, and all that is noble and Christ-like shall abound as the flowers bud and blossom beneath the summer's rain and sun. Then it shall be easy to rejoice in what the Lord does for others, in them, and by them, for this we shall find brings a reflex blessing upon ourselves.

2. We should rejoice in what the Lord does for others, *for their sake.* To joy before God on the behalf of others is to encourage them. As the sun causes the flowers to open and reveal their inner beauty, so encouragement inspires the soul to unfold hidden resources of which we never imagined. As the warm summer's rain causes the grass to sprout with renewed vigour, so encouragement gives a fresh impetus to the child of God in the Divine life, and spurs him on with renewed diligence in the way of the Lord. As the kind word of appreciation spoken by the father in kindly tones begets in the boy a new longing to do something more that shall be pleasing to his parent, so encouragement exerts an influence which shall be as far-reaching as the ever-widening ripples in the water caused by the thrown stone. Let us rejoice in what the Lord does for, in, and by others because of the encouragement it gives to them.

3. We should rejoice in what the Lord does for

others, *for the Lord's sake.* To joy before God on behalf of others is to praise God who is the Author of the cause of our joy. It is said that, when the sun is going out of sight, the pious Swiss herdsman of the Alps takes his Alpine horn, and shouts loudly through it, " Praise ye the Lord." Then a brother herdsman on some distant slope takes up the echo, " Praise ye the Lord." Soon another answers, still higher up the mountains, till hill shouts to hill, and peak echoes to peak, the sublime anthem of praise to the Lord of all. In like manner as we mark what God does for others let us lift up our hearts and voices in praise to the Lord till every member of the body of Christ sends the word on and up to the throne of God.

There is one thing we must not forget to emphasize, and that is the words, "*before our God,*" for this reminds us that our joy on behalf of others is in the Lord's presence, and therefore not for our own sake nor for others' sake as to the primary reason, but for the Lord's sake alone, and as done at His prompting, and for His glory. Three clergymen were once conversing on the subject of praise in relation to themselves. One said, " Give me praise for my preaching because I like it." The second said, " Give me praise that I may give it to my Master." The third said, " Give my Master all the praise, and let me not have any."

III. PRAYER.—" Night and day praying exceedingly that we may see your face." Christmas Evans once said that " prayer is the rope up in the belfry : we pull it, and it rings the bell up in heaven."

Taking the above definition of prayer in relation to what the Apostle here says, we may remark that there are three strands of the rope of his prayer, as illustrating the manner of his pleading.   His prayer was incessant, intense, and importunate.

1. *Incessant.*   " Night and day praying."   The praying of Paul was not of the kind which has been styled as " runaway knocks at heaven's gate," but it was the incessant habit of his spirit, which was as essential to him as the food he ate and as the air he breathed.   One has said, in speaking of four subjects for prayer,—

> " Four things which are not in Thy treasury,
> I lay before Thee, Lord, with this petition :
> My nothingness, my wants,
> My sins, and my contrition."

We have only to know the first, to make us constant in prayer, for if we realize our nothingness, there will always be a need to supply, and a void to be occupied. Oh Christian ! cultivate the holy habit of prayer, so that you may turn to God as instinctively as the needle points to the pole as it is shaken by the motion of the vessel.

2. *Intense.*   " Praying exceedingly."   As diamond will cut diamond, so Scripture will explain Scripture. This is illustrated in relation to the compound Greek word that is rendered " exceeding " as demonstrating the intensity of the Apostle's pleading.   In Daniel iii. 23 we read that the place into which the three Hebrew young men were cast was a " burning fiery furnace."   Now in the Greek Version of the Old Testament we have the same compound word used

in describing the intensity of the fire into which the young men were cast as Paul uses in speaking of his praying. In Eph. iii. 20 Paul uses the same compound word again, in speaking of the more than abundant answer that God gives to those who are abiding in the prescribed condition, when he says, "Now unto Him that is able to do exceeding abundantly above all that we ask or think, according to the power that worketh in us." "Some illustrations strike the eye as well as the ear, and we are thus enabled to reach the mind through those two channels at once. Suppose, here is a tumbler filled with water, so full that it probably would accommodate scarce another drop. Now, the Greeks would have called that by a word that means 'fulness.' Suppose I continue to pour into this tumbler and it overflows : that would call for another expression, 'over-fulness.' Suppose I continue to pour until the overflow exhausts the pitcher and drenches the floor, the Greek would call that 'an excess beyond over-fulness.' That is exactly the expression that is used here. The first word means an excess, the prefix means an excess of an excess, and the whole expression means an excess of an excess of an excess. That is what Paul says about prayer—'Now unto Him that is able to do excessively and super-excessively and super-super-excessively.' That is the God you have to deal with. He can not only fill your little measure till it overflows, but He can pour in upon the overflow, and still upon the overflow of the overflow continue to pour in."

As the furnace was a burning fiery one into which

the Hebrew young men were cast, so the Apostle prayed with the intensity of a raging and fiery furnace. As the Holy Spirit uses the most extraordinary language, "the excess of the overflow of abundance," in speaking of the measure of God's answer to prayer, so the Apostle prayed in such a manner that his prayer was the *intense of the intense of the intensity of prayer.* How many of us have got up to boiling point, leaving out the superlativeness of the superlativeness of prayer ?

3. *Importunate.* "That we may see your face." The one and repeated prayer of Paul and his companions, in spite of the hindering of Satan, was, that they might see the young Christians at Thessalonica. These servants of God did not leave off praying, because they were not answered at once, but they pleaded the more because they were kept waiting. Should this not encourage and stimulate us to plead with holy importunity, till the righteous and loving Lord answers our plea, as the unjust judge did that of the widow, and as the friend was constrained to give the loaf of bread to his persevering neighbour?

IV. FAITH.—" And may perfect that which is lacking in your faith." It is important that we should understand the meaning of the word " perfect " in this verse in relation to the subject of faith. This word " perfect " means to " readjust," to " restore." It is used in surgical language of the setting of a bone or joint, and of repairing nets, also of refitting and strengthening ships. Eadie says, " The verb signifies to refit or readjust literally; then, ethically, to restore ; then to fill up, to supply, or to finish thoroughly." The term is used in Matt. iv. 21, in calling attention to the fact that James and John were "*mending* their nets" when Christ called them; and in Gal. vi. 1 we find that the spiritually-minded believer is to seek to "*restore*" the brother who has been overtaken by a fault. There were lackings in the faith of those to whom the Apostle was writing, which had need to be supplied, even as a disabled ship is in need of repair. To quote Dr. Eadie once more:—"Their faith was not perfect, it was lacking in some elements. It needed to grow in compass, to embrace yet more elements of doctrine, and have a firmer and more harmonious hold of truths already taught, such as the Second Advent. Their faith was also lacking in power; it had not led them to a universal obedience, or given them strength to surmount all heathen propensities and impurities, as is implied in the following chapter. Nor had its influence descended into every-day life in its secular aspects, enforcing honest industry and ennobling it." Their faith seemed to be lacking in several directions, but specially in three:—in not having thrown off all the old habits formed in sin (1 Thess. iv. 1-6); in neglecting their daily vocation, thus being idle, and in consequence misrepresenting the Gospel towards those who were ungodly (1 Thess. iv. 10-12); and in not being well grounded in relation to the coming of Christ (1 Thess. iv. 13, 14). Is our faith lacking in any one particular? If so, let us through grace supply the want.

Let us take three simple illustrations, which may help us to see if our faith is strong in every part.

Faith is like a straight line, like a circle, and like a triangle.

Faith is like a straight line, for it takes the ruler of the Word of God, and causes the life to correspond thereto. If there is any crookedness in the home life, in the business life, in the social life, in the church life, in the citizen life, or in the private life, it is because the Word of God has not been taken and the life made to correspond to it. Would there be uncleanness in the heart, corruption in the state, worldliness in the Church, unholy alliance with un-believers, dishonest practice in the business, or loose-ness in the home, if we in faith took the Word of God, and sought to regulate everything by its direc-tions? We know right well there would not. If we are lacking in any one part of our life as Christians, it is because we are lacking in our faith in God.

Faith is like a circle, for as all that is in the circle is included within it, so faith draws a circle right round our life, and excludes all that is not of God, and includes all that is of Him. It was because Abram was in this circle of faith that he would not receive the riches of Sodom from the hands of its king. It was because Moses was in this circle that he separated from Egypt with all its pleasures and wisdom. " Walk circumspectly," said the Apostle; that is, let the whole life be as a circle, so that those who are without may see no part wanting in the walk as a child of God.

Faith is like a triangle. Upon one side of the triangle we read, THE DEPOSIT OF FAITH, and the words, " I know Him whom I have believed, and am persuaded that He is able to keep that which I have committed unto Him against that day." Upon the bottom of the triangle we read, THE DELIGHT OF FAITH, and the words, "I delight to do Thy will, O my God." And upon the remaining side of the triangle we read, THE DECLARATION OF FAITH, and the words, "I am not ashamed of the Gospel of Christ; for it is the power of God unto salvation, to every one that believeth; to the Jew first, and also to the Greek. For therein is the righteousness of God revealed from faith to faith; as it is written, The just shall live by faith."

Is there any part of our faith lacking as seen in the light of these illustrations? Have we committed ourselves and all we have and are into the Lord's keeping? Our hearts, our heads, our hands, our feet, our time, our talents, our reputation, our cares, our troubles, our work, our children, our money, our all? Are these deposited in the heavenly bank? If they are not, our faith is lacking in an all-round confidence in God. Do we delight in God's Word? Is that our guide? Are His ways our paths? Is His glory our aim? Is His truth our joy? Is His love our motive power? Is His Spirit the element in which we live and move? If not, our faith is lacking. Do we give a clear and faithful declaration as to the truth of the Gospel? Is our witness heard? Or do we hide our light under the bed of indolence, or smother it by the bushel of commerce? If we do, we need to be put into the dock of penitence, and to humble ourselves under the mighty hand of God, that He may repair us, and fit us to be faithful witnesses, fearless watchmen, and full of faith like Abraham; that we may give glory to God, and be a power for Him, even as Abraham was as he moved up and down confessing that he was a stranger and a pilgrim on the earth, and that he sought a city whose Builder and Maker was God.

DIRECTION

"Now may our God and Father Himself, and our Lord Jesus, direct our way unto you" (1 Thess. 3:11 R.V.)

25

DIRECTION

THE prayers of Paul are like the rainbow, they sweep right across the sky of our life; so that all that pertains to our best interest and God's glory — and God's glory is always to our interest — are comprehended within their circle. His prayers are as varied as the colours of the rainbow. They touch the throne of God and the tent of man. They take in the work of the Spirit in its widest, deepest, and highest range in relation to the saint and his walk; and they point to the welfare of the sinner in urging the servant of God to proclaim the Gospel to him in its freeness and fulness. And the prayers of Paul take in, in their circumference, the purpose of God right on to the eternal ages; and they come down to the details of every-day life in its minutice and difficulties, as we see in the verse before us, in Paul's praying to be directed to the saints that he longed to see.

Not a thing was too small or insignificant, in the estimation of Paul, for the Lord's direction. Whether it be in taking a journey or sending a brother on one, he seeks the guidance and will of God. Should not the same dependence be seen in us ? For, as Ruskin says, " there is nothing so small but that we may honour God by asking His guidance of it, or insult Him by taking it into our own hands."

I. THE DIRECTOR.—" Now may our God and Father Himself, and our Lord Jesus, direct our way unto you." It is interesting to note the unity of the Godhead here. The verb " direct," belonging to both persons, is in the singular number. The direction of the Father is the direction of the Son ; the love of the Son is the love of the Father; the word of the Father is the word of the Son ; the works of the Son are the works of the Father ; the bestowment of the Father is the gift of the Son ; and *vice versâ* in each case. What confidence it should beget in our hearts as we remember that God, the Almighty One, is our Father, and the Lord of all is our Saviour ! This is the God who is willing to direct our way as we seek His guidance by prayer, and confide in Him by faith.

II. THE DIRECTING.—The answer to the prayer of the Apostle was deferred, but five years afterwards it was given in his return to Macedonia. The question is naturally asked by many, when the leading of the Lord is referred to, " How may I know when I have the Lord's direction ?" When the following four things focus, we may be sure that the Lord is leading us in a given direction.

First, *We must be in close touch with the Lord.* It is a sad confession that king Saul made to Samuel as he came forth from the unseen world to answer his inquiry about the kingdom of Israel : " I am sore distressed; for the Philistines make war against me, and God is departed from me, and answereth me no more, neither by prophets nor by dreams" (1 Sam. xxviii. 15). As the hand loses the sense of touch if paralysis seizes hold of it, so when the spirit becomes benumbed by the influences of the world, we lose our sensitiveness as to the leading of the Spirit through having grieved Him. But if, on the other hand, we are in close and abiding communion with God, we shall at once know His will, even as the sensitive paper of the photographer receives the impression.

Second, *We must remember that the Lord never guides contrary to His Word.* We have known some who have professed to be led by the Lord, who have been acting in direct opposition to His Word. We have no hesitation in saying that they have been as much deceived as the prophet who was led astray by the old prophet of Bethel. The incident of the disobedient prophet is full of interest as illustrating how we must be led by the Word of God alone on the one hand, and what may be the consequence of obeying *a supposed word of God* on the other hand. The prophet out of Judah had received instructions to go to Bethel and pronounce judgment against Jeroboam and his idolatry. He was obedient so far, and the Lord attested his fidelity by rending the altar. When Jeroboam heard his message he would have laid hold of him, but God caused the king's hand to wither; then Jeroboam entreated the man of God to pray that his hand might be restored, and he did so, and God heard the prayer. Then the king asked him to go home with him and have some refreshment and receive a reward; but the servant of God, remembering his directions, said, " If thou wilt give me half thine house, I would not go in with thee, neither will I eat bread nor drink water in this place : for so was it charged me by the word of the Lord, saying, Eat no bread, nor drink water, nor turn again by the same way that thou camest" (1 Kings xiii. 8, 9). The prophet leaves Bethel, and makes for his home by another way.   Now there is at Bethel an old prophet who has two sons, and these two sons go home and tell their father what they have heard the man of God say to the king.   The old prophet, hearing the way the man of God has gone, saddles his ass and goes after him.   He finds him sitting under an oak tree, and he seeks to get him to go back to Bethel.   By telling a lie in saying he has received a message from the Lord that he was to do so, he succeeds.   What is the result ?   While the man of God is sitting at the table of the old prophet eating and drinking, the word of God comes to the latter.   "And he cried unto the man of God that came from Judah, saying, Thus saith the Lord, Forasmuch as thou hast disobeyed the mouth of the Lord, and hast not kept the commandment which the Lord thy God commanded thee, but camest back, and hast eaten bread and drunk water in the place of the which the Lord did say to thee, Eat no bread, and drink no water; thy carcase shall not come unto the sepulchre of thy fathers " (1 Kings xiii. 21, 22).   What is the sequel ? The man of God is slain by a lion.   In the above incident we have a man who acted contrary to the word of God, and the consequence.   The man of God

had received definite directions from the Lord, and it
was for him to keep to them, and not to be deceived
by any supposed message from God. Let us be careful, in seeking guidance from the Lord, that we remember that the Lord never contradicts His word.
If we have "Thus saith the Lord" for the way we
take, we may be sure that the Spirit of the Lord is
guiding us.

Third, *We must have no will of our own in seeking the Lord's direction, but seek His glory alone.*
As the piece of wood is in the power of the carpenter,
and he can do as he wills with it, and make that
which is in his mind, so we need to be submissive
and makeable in the hands of the Divine Carpenter.

> " Lord, might I be but as a saw,
>   A plane, a chisel, in Thy hand ?
> No, Lord, I take it back with awe—
>   Such prayer for me is far too grand.
> I pray, O Master, let me lie
>   As on Thy bench the favoured wood ;
> Thy saw, Thy plane, Thy chisel ply,
>   And work me into something good."

As the mountain climber is lashed to his guide as he
is passing over some dangerous part of the glacier,
and he goes and does as the guide directs, so we
must be lashed with the rope of faith to our Divine
Guide, and He will lead us into safety and peace. As
the head guides and governs the members of the
body, so our Divine Head must rule and regulate us
if we would be His guided ones.

Fourth, *As the Lord directs, all obstacles will be
removed out of the way.* John Newton well says,

" I believe that wherever guidance is honestly and simply sought, it is certainly given. As to our discernment of it, I believe it depends upon the measure in which we are walking in the light. One indulged sin may so cloud the sky that it spreads a mist, so that to see what God is doing is impossible. But neither the casting of lots, the opening of the Bible at a venture, nor the sudden impression of a text, nor freedom in prayer over a matter, nor a dream, furnishes any reliable direction. The Lord rather opens and shuts, throws down the walls of difficulty, or hedges the way with thorns for those who confidently seek His guidance by prayer. They know that their concerns are in His hands, and fear to run before He sends, or to delay when He directs an advance."

PHASES OF LOVE

"And the Lord make you to increase and abound in love one toward another, and toward all men, even as we also *do* toward you" (1 Thess. 3:12 R.V.)

26

PHASES OF LOVE

LIGHT is one as the embodiment of colour. It is as light strikes prismatic forms that the three primary colours appear, and as they mingle the secondary colours are manifest also: even so is love. Love is one, and yet it manifests itself in different ways. Thus in the verse before us we may find nine phases of love.

I. THE SOURCE OF LOVE.—"The Lord." The Lord spoken of is the Lord Jesus. What is said of the Father and the Holy Spirit in their action, is also declared of the Lord Jesus. For instance, the work of creation, while applied to all three persons of the God-head (Gen. 1:26), is stated to have been done by each alike (Gen. 1:2; John 1:3); Acts 17:24). So also is love. God in the Trinity of His personality loves us—and each Person in the Trinity, even as the three primary colours are distinct through the prism, and yet the colours are one in essence. As the beating pulse tells of the throbbing heart, so the loving action speaks of God's love. As the flower in its beauty tells of the sun's painting, so the beautiful life of holy love declares the presence of Him who is Love. As the burning coals remind us of the bottled up sunshine, so the warm deed of compassionate love makes known the indwelling love of God.

II. THE POWER OF LOVE.—"The Lord *make*." It is the abundant rain that causes the river to overflow its banks, and water the surrounding country, as the river Nile in Egypt; even so as the love of God rises in our soul by the Spirit of love we are a blessing to others. It is as the steam fills the vacuum brake upon the train that the brakes are kept off the carriages; even so as the love of God fills us we go on unhindered in the way of godliness. It is as oil is poured upon the fire that it burns more vehemently; even so as the love of God is shed abroad in our hearts by the Holy Spirit we are warmed into devotion and vehement zeal for the glory of God. It is as the sugar mixes with the tea that it is agreeable to our palate; even so the love of God impregnating our whole being makes us like itself, viz., lovely in loving. It is as the salt permeates the meat that it is preserved from corruption; even so as we keep ourselves in the love of God we are preserved from evil. If we are to love it must be the outcome of God's love in us causing us to move in His ways, even as the water turns the wheel which moves the machine to grind the corn.

III. THE PERSONALITY OF LOVE.—"The Lord make *you*," &c. The Lord is always personal in His dealings with us. He who notes the individual sparrow in its fall to the ground is sure to note each one of us in our personal need. It is *one* sinner over whom love rejoices when he repents. It was the *one* piece of silver that the woman diligently sought after; and it was the *one* prodigal that the Father ran to meet. "*I* received mercy," says Paul in speaking of his personal salvation. In like manner the woman of Samaria said to the Samaritans, "Come, see a man that told *me* all things that ever *I* did: is not this the Christ?"

IV. THE PROGRESS OF LOVE.—"The Lord make you to *increase*." As a plant will grow the better if placed in a larger place, so the Lord places us, as the Psalmist says, "in a large room." If we are bound in the pot of prejudice or pride, it will be to our advantage to be placed in the large place of the love of God. As the thick undergrowth will hinder the more delicate trees from growing healthily and vigorously, and the gardener's plan is to cut away the undergrowth, so as the Heavenly Gardener takes from us the undergrowth of worldliness, selfishness, and covetousness we are made to increase in the Divine life of grace. As some plants fail to flourish because of their environment, and the only way for them to increase in growth and beauty is to put them in better surroundings, by placing them in the warm greenhouse, where they are protected from the cold winds; so as we abide in Christ, by living in the consciousness of His presence, we make progress in the Word and ways of God.

V. THE ABOUNDING OF LOVE.—"The Lord make you to increase and *abound* in love." The term "*increase*" seems to refer to the inner life of the believer in Christ, and the word "*abound*," to the outward life of Christian activity,—the overflow of love. It is as the love of God fills our nature that we are like the fruitful vine, which is so surcharged with sap from the richness that it has taken in from the soil, that it breaks forth in abundant fruit for the refreshment and strengthening of mankind.

VI. THE ATMOSPHERE OF LOVE.—"The Lord make you to increase and abound *in love*." The double truth, so often expressed in relation to Christ and His Word, is also brought out in relation to love. We are in Christ as to position, and Christ is in us as to power. We are in the truth as the element in which we move, and the truth is in us as the energy to prompt us in life. We are in the faith as to responsibility as to its teaching, and the faith is in us as the regulator of our walk in the world. In like manner, the love of God is in us as the motive to inspire us, and yet we are to "abound in love" as the atmosphere into which we are to enter more and more, even as the higher the altitude we reach on our earth the greater elasticity we have in walking.

VII. THE EXCLUSIVENESS OF LOVE.—"The Lord make you to increase and abound in love, *one toward another*." We are bound to love all who profess to love our Lord, but we cannot always love some of their ways, even as the Lord finds many things in us which are unlovely, and which call for His condemnation. The new commandment is, that we love one another, and love each other *as* Christ has loved us. Law commanded that we should love others as we love ourselves, but grace directs us to love as Christ loves; and further, that there is to be an increasing and abounding in our love to each other, even as the river increases in volume and force and usefulness as it nears the sea.

VIII. THE INCLUSIVENESS OF LOVE.—" Toward *all men*." We cannot love the world with the *love of complacency*, but we must love it with the *love of compassion*. To love all men with the love of complacency would mean that we find satisfaction in all they are and do, and this can never be to the hater of sin and sinful ways; but we can love all men with the love of compassion in that we seek to bring them to the Lord that He may cleanse them by His blood, and sanctify them by His Spirit. To do this is to be in sympathy with Christ's heart, and to be acting in obedience to His Word.

IX. AN ILLUSTRATION OF LOVE.—" Even as we do toward you." No one can ponder the life and labours of the devoted servants of Christ who sent this epistle, without being impressed with their devotion to Christ, their holy zeal, their patient perseverance, their unfaltering fidelity, their love of the truth, their rejoicing in tribulation, their self-abasement, their constant solicitude for the welfare of others, without acknowledging that they practised what they preached, and illustrated every truth they proclaimed by their lives. Would that the same could be said of all who profess to be servants of Christ! Too often Christ is wounded in the house of His friends by inconsistencies in the lives of those who profess to be His, and young believers are stumbled by the want of conformity to Christ and His Word of those who should be examples of the flock.   When we can say there is a correspondence between our lips and lives, then we are like the full moon, which reflects without any earth shadow the glory of the sun.

A FIXED HEART

" To the end He may stablish your hearts unblameable in holiness before God, even our Father, at the coming of our Lord Jesus Christ with all His saints" (**1 Thess. 3:13 A.V.**)

27

A FIXED HEART

AGAIN and again do we find the Psalmist praying for a "fixed heart." What does this mean? A fixed heart means a constant heart— "Renew a right" (margin, "constant," or "fixed") "spirit within me" (Psalm 51:10). A fixed heart means a communing heart. "My heart is fixed, O God, my heart is fixed" (Psalm 57:7; 108:1). A fixed heart is a confiding heart. "His heart is fixed, trusting in the Lord" (Psalm 112:7). As it is said of Rehoboam that "he did evil, because he prepared" (margin, "fixed") "not his heart to seek the Lord" (2 Chron. 12:14), and that was the cause of all his evil doing, so, on the other hand, the one whose heart is fixed has the secret of growth in grace, of doing good to others, and of bringing glory to God. What do we understand by the heart believing and loving? It seems to include the assent of the understanding, the consent of the will, and the accent of the affections. Thus a heart fixed on the Lord means the assent of our understanding to His truth, the consent of our will to His will, and the accent of our love to put Him first and foremost in all things.

We have the characteristics of a fixed heart in the verse before in seven particulars.

I. A FIXED HEART IS AN ACQUIESCING HEART.— *" To the end,"* &c. We enter into the purpose of God, in that we allow Him to make us abound in love, so that we apprehend as we love each other and all men, our heart is fixed; thus we enter into the plan of God, even as the obedient child has fellowship with its mother, in obeying her. As Eadie says, " Love tends to confirm, for it is the bond of perfectness. When the heart is filled with love to brethren, and to mankind, it becomes established; it rises beyond the sphere of doubts and oscillations, for it is fulfilling the law, and growing in that holiness which such love sustains and develops." As the oxygen causes the fire to burn as the lighted match ignites the well-arranged wood, paper, and coals in the fire-grate; so, as there is on our part the acquiescence in the Divine plan, the Lord is able in the breath of His Spirit to fuse our hearts into one glowing mass of love.

II. A FIXED HEART IS A GOVERNED HEART.—" To the end *He,"* &c. It will be observed in the verse before us, and the two preceding it, that prominence is given to the fact that the Lord Himself is the Great Worker, even as the water moves the water wheel of the mill, and that in turn moves all the machinery. The Lord is said to be the *Director* in verse eleven, the *Empowerer* in verse twelve, and the *Establisher* in verse thirteen. As in salvation from the guilt of sin we apprehend that it was of the

Lord alone, even so in growth in grace and fixedness of heart it must be the Lord who rules and governs. The government of our being must be upon the shoulder of our Lord, even as the magnet keeps the needle to itself by its own inherent power.

III. A FIXED HEART IS AN ESTABLISHED HEART.— " May *stablish*," &c. This is almost like saying " a fixed heart is a fixed heart." But let us remember that by repetition we may seize the attention, even as the repeated blows of the hammer will weld the pieces of hot iron together. There are two mighty factors that the Lord uses to establish His children ; these are His truth and His grace. We are exhorted to be " rooted and built up in Him, and stablished in the faith " (Col. ii. 7). Here are two illustrations used in speaking of steadfastness in the truth, namely, the tree well rooted and the building substantially grounded. If we are grounded in the truth, like the house built into the rock, we are safe in all storms of temptation, and if we are securely rooted in the soil of the eternal verities of Jehovah, we shall stand against all the tempests of persecution. It is also declared that " It is a good thing that the heart be established by grace " (Heb. xiii. 9, compare R.V.). If the heart is established in grace it will be like those insects which become the same colour as the thing upon which they feed, as may be seen in the common green fly.

IV. A FIXED HEART IS AN UNBLAMEABLE HEART.— " Unblameable," &c. " Unblameable " means " without reproach," but it does not necessarily signify without fault. The amateur painter makes many mistakes which the skilled eye soon detects; thus he is not without fault, but the novice is free from blame if he has done his best. In like manner, the Lord can always discover defects within us, thus we can never be without fault; but if we are true to the light the Lord has given us, then we are free from blame, even as the Apostle Paul could say of himself and his fellow-labourers (1 Thess. ii. 10), and as he also exhorts these saints to be till the coming of the Lord (1 Thess. v. 23).

V. A FIXED HEART IS A SEPARATED HEART.— "Unblameable in *holiness.*" The meaning of the word "holy" is "separate." We are separated from an unclean and a common use to the service of God, and for His occupation. "*In* holiness" reminds us that holiness is the sphere in which we are to move, even as Aaron and his sons were separated as priests to the Lord and for His service, and in His service they were thenceforth to live and act. A separate heart is like the holiest of all in the tabernacle; it is for God's indwelling alone. And as the presence of God in the burning bush in the wilderness made holy the bush and the surrounding ground, so the heart in which God abides in His holy temple, as He Himself says, "The temple of God is holy, and such are ye" (1 Cor. iii. 16, R.V., margin).

VI. A FIXED HEART IS AN OPEN HEART.—"*Before God, even our Father.*" If we live in the consciousness of the Lord's presence, then we have an open heart. Anything that we seek to hide from the Lord indicates a closed heart, that is, we would that we could act apart from Him. The opened heart is like the uncovered mirror, which reflects the image of the person looking into it; even so, as we with unveiled face gaze upon the glory of the Lord, we are transformed into the same image.

VII. A FIXED HEART WILL BE A MANIFESTED HEART.—" At the coming of our Lord Jesus Christ with all His saints." We generally find that rewards are associated with Christ's coming *with*—and not with His coming *for*—His people. It seems that the reason for this is, that when we are manifested with Christ it will then be seen how faithful we have been, by the position we occupy. That there will be a diversity of position is clearly indicated in Revelation xix., where Christ is seen coming forth at the head of a great army. Now the very thought of an army suggests a diversity of rank. As the medals upon the breast of the soldier speak of the battles in which he has fought, and the honour his sovereign has put upon him in consequence, so when our Lord is manifest in His glory, others shall admire the glory He has put upon us, because of our achievements through Him (2 Thess. i. 10).